Prince of Dublin Printers

Prince of Dublin Printers

THE LETTERS OF
GEORGE FAULKNER

Robert E. Ward

The University Press of Kentucky

ISBN: 978-0-8131-6039-9

Library of Congress Catalog Card Number: 71-160053

Copyright © 1972 by The University Press of Kentucky

A statewide cooperative scholarly publishing agency
serving Berea College, Centre College of Kentucky,
Eastern Kentucky University, Kentucky Historical Society,
Kentucky State College, Morehead State University, Murray
State University, University of Kentucky, University of
Louisville, and Western Kentucky University.

Editorial and Sales Offices: Lexington, Kentucky 40506

To Curt A. Zimansky

Contents

Preface

Although George Faulkner corresponded with Swift, Pope, Johnson, and Lord Chesterfield, all his letters to these men are no longer extant. For example, R. W. Chapman, *Letters of Samuel Johnson* (Oxford: Clarendon Press, 1952), 1:55; 2:29, mentions definite correspondence between Faulkner and Johnson, yet could not find a single letter. Harold Williams prints several letters of Swift to Faulkner, yet could not find any of Faulkner's letters to Swift. Also Bonamy Dobree, the latest Chesterfield editor (*The Letters of Philip Dormer Stanhope*, 4th Earl of Chesterfield, ed. Bonamy Dobree, 6 vols. [London: Eyre and Spottiswoode, 1932]), could not find any Faulkner letters to Chesterfield. Thus, the letters written by these men to Faulkner do not appear to be extant. Those that are extant are letters to minor literary and political figures. Their letters, printed here in their entirety for the first time, give an unprecedented view of Anglo-Irish social and political events, as well as a view of the Anglo-Irish printer-publisher at work.

The text of the following letters has been transcribed from facsimile copies of the original letters. No changes have been made in either spelling or punctuation. Difficult readings of words or sentences have been rendered in brackets. Crossed out words or sentences have also been enclosed in brackets and footnoted. An example of such procedure may be noted in George Faulkner's letter to Charles O'Conor on 7 November 1766. Faulkner wrote a line about Dr. Johnson's laziness which he later crossed out. This letter and several others would appear to be first drafts and the changing thoughts of the writer are important to the reader as bibliographer and literary historian.

This book would not be possible without the following permissions: the letters of George Faulkner to Samuel Derrick by courtesy of the Victoria and Albert Museum, London, England; the letters from George Faulkner to Charles O'Conor of Belanagare by courtesy of the Royal Irish Academy, Dublin, Ireland; the letters of Charles O'Conor to George Faulkner by permission of the Trustees of the British Museum, London, England; a letter from George Faulkner to Edmund Burke by permission of Earl Fitzwilliam and the Northamptonshire Record Office, Delapre Abbey, Northampton, England; a portion of a letter from George Faulkner to Lord Orrery by permission of the Harvard College Library, Cambridge, Massachusetts; two letters of George Faulkner to William Bowyer and an anonymous person by permission of Mrs. Donald Hyde, and the Hyde Collection, Somerville, New Jersey; a letter from George Faulkner to the Earl of Orrery by permission of the Master and Fellows of Trinity College, Cambridge University.

I am further indebted to the following publishers and university presses for permission to quote from these sources: *The Correspondence of Jonathan Swift*, ed. Harold Williams, Vols. IV and V; *The Correspondence of Alexander Pope*, ed. George Sherburn, Vols. I and IV; *The Letters of Samuel Johnson*, ed. R. W. Chapman, Vol. 1; *The Poems of Jonathan Swift*, Vol. III; all by permission of Clarendon Press, Oxford. *The Prose Works of Jonathan Swift*, ed. Herbert Davis, Vol. XIII, by permission of Basil Blackwell, Publisher; Robert L. Munter, *The History of the Irish Newspaper, 1685–1760*, by permission of the Cambridge University Press; W. E. H. Lecky, *A History of Ireland in the Eighteenth Century*, Vols. I and II, courtesy of AMS Press, Inc.; Anthony Ashley Cooper, Third Earl of Shaftesbury, *Characteristics of Men, Manners, Opinions, and Times*, ed. John M. Robertson, by permission of Peter Smith, Publisher; Herbert Teerink, *A Bibliography of the Works of Jonathan Swift*, ed. Arthur Scouten, by permission of the University of Pennsylvania Press; and the following members of the American Association of University Presses, from whose books I have quoted: Yale University Press, for Ronald Paulson, *The*

Graphic Works of William Hogarth, Vol. I; Princeton University Press for Lewis M. Knapp, *Tobias Smollett: Doctor of Men and Letters*; Southern Illinois University Press for *London Stage, 1660–1800*, ed. G. W. Stone, Vol. II, Part IV; University of North Carolina Press for Allan D. McKillop, *Samuel Richardson: Printer and Novelist*; University of Texas Press for Reginald H. Griffith, *Alexander Pope: A Bibliography*, Vol. I, Parts 1 and 2.

Acknowledgment should be made to Professor Lowell Harrison, who has overseen the development of this book, and to President Dero Downing and the Board of Regents of Western Kentucky University for funding this book.

A Sketch of George Faulkner

GEORGE FAULKNER'S Dublin was a city of grandeur, music, and dramatic activity; in contrast it was also a city of filth, violence, and vice. For fifty years (1725–1775) Faulkner's *Dublin Journal* mirrored all the magnificence, turbulence, gaiety, and heartbreak of eighteenth-century Dublin. The city's love of show reached its culmination in the viceregal pomp of celebration when all Dublin followed the Lord Lieutenant (Faulkner's friend, the Earl of Chesterfield) in celebration of the king's birthday. George Faulkner described the decorations for the birthday of George II on 30 October 1745:

The Square of the Castle being finely painted new and the Gate leading to the lower Castle was a triumphal Arch and very finely painted, and over that the King's Arm's with a Profile of his Majesty on the right Side and that of the Prince of Wales on the Left, all properly emblazoned on Muslin with Lamps behind, which made the most beautiful Appearance. On each Window of the Castle were the Letters GR with a Crown above them and 38 Lamps burning to each. In the Centre of the Building on the right Wing were the Arms of the Earl of Chesterfield; and on the Left those of his Countess, the Countess of Walsingham in her own Right, properly coloured with Lamps burning before them. The Supper Room was all decorated in the most beautiful Manner with fine Paintings, Illuminations, and Statues, the Entrance into it having a Temple of Minerva in the Pediment of which was a *basso relievo* of his Majesty to which the Motto was *Parcere Subjectis Debellare Superbas*. Within the Temple there rose a large and beautiful Obelisk which seemed all one Blaze of Light from the Number of wax Tapers which illuminated it; and over the Side-board which surrounded the inside of the Temple at a proper Height quite around were several Statues which poured a perpetual Flow of the choicest Wines of all Sorts into nick Basins properly placed to receive them, from whence the Liquor was conveyed into the lower Castle Yard where it played off in several Fountains of Wine during the Whole of the Entertainment to give the Populace an Opportunity to drink his Majesty's Health and long Life, and Confusion to his Enemies.[1]

Besides regal pomp there was also music, dear to the hearts of the Dubliners. Musical fare at the Music Hall in Fishamble

Street came directly from London. George Friedrich Handel, unable to get a London hearing for his new Oratorio *The Messiah*, had brought it to Dublin. Faulkner took proper notice of "Mr. Handel's Performance of his Oratorio, call'd the *Messiah* for the Support of Hospitals and other pious Uses at the Musick Hall in Fishamble Street, on Tues. April 13, 1742 before the Lords Justices, and a vast Assembly of the Nobility and Gentry of both Sexes."[2]

Dublin's Music Hall also had presented John Milton's *Comus* with incidental music written by the Englishman Thomas Arne on 11 January 1742/43.[3] Other theaters too presented musical entertainment. Faulkner advertised in his *Dublin Journal* one of many performances of the *Beggar's Opera* at Thomas Sheridan's Smock Alley Theater on 23 March 1746/47.[4]

Life for the rich or well-to-do citizen was glittering and entertaining, but it was quite different for the poor tradesman printer, the criminal, or the Catholic. If the tradesman were lucky he might become a member of the Common Council.[5] The libel laws were vague and since they were vague they were constantly being broken. It was essentially a matter of whether someone wished to prosecute. Arrest on the charge of public libel could be financially ruinous. An example of this appeared in Faulkner's *Dublin Journal*: "Last Saturday, Henry Bade, a Printer, who was last Term convicted for printing a false, scandalous, and malicious Libel [against] Sir John Freke, bart., and Ensign John Perry Cooke, stood in the Pillory, opposite the Tholstel, pursuant to his Sentence, the last Day of Last Term, and was afterwards carried back to Newgate where he now lies."[6]

Dublin had its share of filthy prisons such as the Newgate or the Marshalsea. Faulkner's commentaries in his newspaper about jail fever during the hot summer weather in Dublin brought the following comment from a concerned Dubliner: "As to what you have said in regards to keeping Prisons and Prisoners clean, I think it highly worthy the Consideration of the Publick, especially at this Time; for as Dr. Mead justly remarks, that nothing approacheth so near to the first Original of Contagion, as Air pent, loaded with Damps, and

4

corrupted with Filthiness, that proceeds from animal Bodies; and he further says that what they call Jail Fever, is always attended with a Degree of Malignity in proportion to the Closeness and Stench of the Place." [7]

Death could also come as a result of wagon accidents in the streets of eighteenth-century Dublin. Faulkner complained about the suburban streets: "Many Complaints have been made of late of the Badness of the Roads leading to Dublin, particularly of those near the Suburbs by which several wheel Carriages are overturned and Hay and Straw are much damaged, many Limbs broken and Riders thrown from their Horses. Query, who is to mend these Roads, which are commonly the worst near the Toll and Custom Houses? And how is the Money applied that is collected at these Places?" [8]

Other accidents occurred because of the lack of lighting on the city streets. Such a problem caused the Irish Parliament to pass a law which laid responsibility for lighting areas of the city on the various church parishes. Faulkner printed in his *Journal* a letter to the editor concerning this:

The insufficient Lighting of the Streets of Dublin was complained of as a great Grievance, and the Occasion of the Committing many Robberies and other heinous Crimes; to remedy which Mischief an Act passed last Session, directing that the Lamps shall be kept lighted and burning from Sunset to Sunrising during the whole Year and that the Lamplighter should attend all Night to keep the Lamps constantly lighted and that upon any Complaint made to the Church Wardens of any Neglect of Duty in the Contractors for Lighting the Lamps or the Lamplighters, they are required immediately to summon them and the Witnesses one each side to the Vestry Room of the Parish and examine into the Neglect on Oath and if it shall appear that there has been any Neglect, the Contractors shall forfeit such Sum as the Church Wardens shall deem just and reasonable, which Sum will be deducted out of the Wages of the Contractor and applied for the Lighting of the Lamps. [9]

Besides minor problems like lighting and street repairs, there appeared one unsolvable problem. Land enclosure for grazing forced many country people off the land and into the cities as beggars or thieves. This enclosure movement caused trouble in the suburbs of Dublin. Faulkner complained, "the many Riots and Robberies in and near Dublin are attributed to the Enclosure of the Fields and Gardens round this Town where all Degrees of People formerly had the Liberty of Walking for Business, Ease, and Safety to and fro, and where they used to wrestle, play at Hurley, pitching of Quoits, Football and other healthy Amusements." [10]

These pictures of the glamour, the violence, and the poverty of the provincial capital appeared in George Faulkner's *Dublin Journal*. Its editor gained fame not only locally as editor of the *Journal* but also historically as Jonathan Swift's "Prince of Dublin Printers." [11]

Like Jonathan Swift, George Faulkner was Anglo-Irish, born in Dublin. The date of his birth is uncertain, but most sources give it as 1699. His father was a butcher and a member of the Established Church. Little is known of his mother except that she had distant connections with the noble Dillon family. [12] There is little specific information concerning Faulkner's early years. He attended the academy of the Reverend Dr. Lloyd, reputed to be "the best preceptor in the Kingdom." [13] After receiving an average classical education, Faulkner, at age fourteen, became apprenticed to Thomas Hume, printer. [14] Hume ran a newspaper, the *Dublin Courant*, where, doubtless, Faulkner helped read copy and learned page makeup. [15] At the end of his apprenticeship Faulkner proposed marriage to Hume's daughter, but she rejected his offer. The young journeyman, realizing there was little work for him in Dublin, migrated to London and the print shop of William Bowyer, Sr. Sometime between 1721 and 1724, Faulkner made the acquaintance of William Bowyer, Jr., the Cambridge-trained printer who supervised the printing of the classics for his father. [16]

In 1724 George Faulkner returned to Dublin to set up his own printing business. [17] He made arrangements to purchase the titles of two newspapers, the *Dublin Journal* and the *Dublin Post Boy*. He printed his first issue of the *Dublin Journal* on 27 March 1725 and his first issue of the *Post Boy* during Christmas week 1725. Faulkner must have prospered at his Pembroke Court-Castle Street address because he went to London in the summer of 1726 "on his own Business and private Affairs."[18] At this time, it seems, Faulkner married a Mrs. Taylor, an English widow, whom he met in London. The time or place of the marriage ceremony is unknown.[19]

Near the end of August Faulkner moved from Pembroke Court to Christ Churchyard.[20] A year later he took into partnership James Hoey, a Catholic printer who had no formal training in the craft.[21] The partners moved their shop in 1729 to "the Pamphlet Shop, opposite the Tholstel." Despite a prosperous business Faulkner and Hoey dissolved their partnership, possibly in April 1730. When Faulkner printed Jonathan Swift's *Vindication of Lord Cartaret . . .* he had already moved to Essex Street, leaving Hoey in Skinners Row.[22] A war of printed insults followed as Hoey spread rumors that Faulkner was giving up printing the *Dublin Journal.* When Faulkner left for England, one step ahead of government prosecution for public libel, Hoey spread the rumor that Faulkner would not return.[23] An extended absence from 2 September until 12 June 1731 gave credence to the rumor. A possible explanation appears in the cautious statement Faulkner printed in his *Journal* when he returned in June. He maintained that he was delayed "by a dangerous and tedious indisposition."[24] Although no date is given by Faulkner's biographer as to the accident which cost him his leg, the biographer does say that the accident occurred on Faulkner's second trip to England:

Before he embarked he had received a slight hurt on one of his shins, which he disregarded so much, that on his going on board the vessel, he put on his boots, and did not pull them off till his arrival in London; he then found his error in not having paid a proper attention to his hurt, for the journey had so inflamed it to so violent a degree that the best assistance could not prevent a Gangrene, which spread so rapidly, that he had no other means of saving his life, but by the loss of his limb.[25]

The loss of his leg did not hinder Faulkner in maintaining a printing business. In a city of approximately a hundred thousand people he kept pace with his major competitors: James Hoey, George Grierson, the Exshaws, the Ewings, Peter Wilson, and Samuel Fairbrother. During Faulkner's lifetime 264 printers and booksellers opened their shops in Dublin;[26] the majority of these ventures failed. Yet George Faulkner succeeded because of his determination, personality, and shrewd business sense. Few Dublin booksellers would dare to scold the reading public for its bad buying habits and then coax it to "come into a subscription to take four books per Annum such as they shall chuse, at three and six-pence per book, at an average, which will amount in all but to four-teen shillings a year, though a very inconsiderable sum to each individual, and little exceeding four bottles of claret, amounts in the whole to twenty-eight thousand pounds; out of which sum we, upon the faith of Christians, desire the small profit of eight thousand."[27]

Besides his ability in getting customers to subscribe for new books, Faulkner was adept in figuring new ways to pack more news and advertising into his paper. He declared that "we are obliged to make use of a smaller letter hitherto, by which this paper is made to contain (besides the advertise-ments) much more news than any other printed in this city is now capable of."[28] A popular newspaper such as the *Dublin Journal* was considered a source of wealth, averaging £ 100–200 advertising revenue annually. Faulkner profited at least £ 900 a year from his advertising in the 1740s.[29]

Faulkner's preference for a type called Elzevir prompted many of his competitors to call him the "oaken-footed Elzevir" and to laugh at his "wooden understanding."[30] But if his understanding was wooden, so was his counte-nance. Faulkner never showed any emotion; Lord Orrery pointed out to a friend that Faulkner had "a solemnity of face that never alters; so that in his brightest or most gloomy hours, he remains immovable in countenance and appears a kind of talking statue."[31] Another idiosyncrasy of Faulkner was his love of fine dress. This caused him often to be the butt of Dean Swift's wit:

Mr. Faulkner being sent for by the dean on some business, put on a gold lace waistcoat; being introduced, the dean affected not to know him, and asked him, "Who he was?" He answered, "I am Faulkner, your printer, Mr. dean." "No," said the dean, "my printer is a plain honest citizen, and you sir, are a fop." Mr.

Faulkner took the hint and withdrew, and returned a short time after in a plain dress, when the dean received him with great freedom, told him "there had been a person who attempted to personate him, but that he was not to be imposed on."[32]

Swift's treatment of George Faulkner did not hurt the printer's sensibilities. On the other hand, Swift's treatment of political issues caused Faulkner a great deal of mental anguish. On 26 February 1731/32 Faulkner printed the substance of a pamphlet by Jonathan Swift in the *Dublin Journal*. Since there was insufficient time to print the pamphlet, titled *Considerations upon Two Bills . . . Relating to the Clergy of Ireland*, before the Irish Parliament voted on the measures, Swift summarized his arguments so that they would more effectively alert both Houses to a scheme by the bishops to create a larger voting block of new priests. If the bills passed, Swift felt the already powerful group of bishops in the House of Lords would have its equivalent in the House of Commons. Swift asked:

Whether the House of Commons may not think the Bishops have power enough already?
Whether a Gentleman would not rather have a credible Parson or a Beggar to converse with?
Whether this Scheme of multiplying beggarly Clergymen, may not by their Numbers, have great Influence on Elections, Being entirely under the Dependence of their Bishops?
Whether a Clause against a Parson's having Votes should not be inserted?
Whether Gentlemen and Farmers would not be easier in their Tythes with a rich Minister than a poor one?
For a hungry Louse biteth sore, etc.[33]

The measure was defeated. It is highly probable that this statement in Faulkner's paper helped defeat the measure. Consequently, the bishops of the House of Lords angrily swore out a warrant for Faulkner's arrest on the charges of public libel. Faulkner quickly learned that printing material which concerned public figures, whether true or false, violated the public peace. Such violation was considered grounds for arrest.[34]

Faulkner appeared before the House of Lords approximately two days after the defeat of the Clergy bill. As Swift told Lord Oxford, Faulkner "suffered severely in his private Property as well as in his Health."[35] His censure from the House of Lords remained in effect until he petitioned for forgiveness and paid an unknown amount of money in fines.[36]

Still smarting from his recent arrest, Faulkner received Swift's gratitude in the form of assignments of printing rights to many of his works. When Mathew Pilkington, Swift's secretary, assigned these rights to Faulkner and William Bowyer, Jr., Swift's friend Alexander Pope complained that Faulkner and Bowyer were turning these assignments into "properties."[37]

Swift's increased confidence in Faulkner no doubt caused him to dream of printing a collection of Swift's works, a project considered impossible by London publishers. Faulkner stated in his *Journal* that "this can nowhere be done so conveniently as in Ireland, whose Booksellers cannot pretend to any Property in what to publish either by Law or Custom."[38] Despite Swift's vacillating attitude, Faulkner started printing four subscription volumes. One example of the Dean's cooperative mood was his letter to Faulkner concerning *Gulliver's Travels*. He commented, "Since you intend to print a new edition of that book, I must tell you that the English printer made several alterations which I much disapprove of."[39]

Benjamin Motte, Swift's London bookseller, became uneasy when he learned of the forthcoming Faulkner edition because Swift appeared to him to be editing Faulkner's edition, thereby making it more authoritative. Even so, neither Motte nor Faulkner knew what Swift's attitude was toward this edition. Swift's irresolution appeared in his letter to the second Earl of Oxford when he introduced Faulkner as "the Prince of Dublin Printers" and then commented, "he is engaged in a work that very much discontents me, yet I would rather have it fall in his hands, than any others on this side."[40]

Meanwhile, Jonathan Swift introduced Faulkner to another person in England, Viscount Bolingbroke; Bolingbroke, however, replied negatively: "If I can do Mr. Faulkner any service, I shall certainly do it . . . , but my help in a project of subscription will, I fear avail him little."[41] Although Faulkner received little help from Bolingbroke, he did receive subscriptions from several noblemen in England. Faulkner replied to an order from Theophilus, Earl of Huntingdon, "Your Lordship may have the two sets of Swift's Works. . . I have published proposals for two volumes more of his writings, and should be proud of the honour of your name in my list of subscribers."[42]

Notwithstanding delays, Faulkner could say on 27 November 1734 that his first three volumes of Swift's *Works* would be ready for delivery on that date. Several difficulties still plagued him: he could not get the books bound fast enough, and he had a problem in distributing five hundred pages of new material. The material became volume four, while *Gulliver's Travels*, originally planned as volume four, became volume three.[43] On 11 January 1734/35 Faulkner announced with pride that his collected edition was finished and ready for sale. He further boasted that "in all other Editions that have been publish'd in London and in Dublin are very many gross Errors and Mistakes . . . so that it may be truly said, a genuine and correct Edition of this Author's Works was never publish'd till this time."[44]

Samuel Fairbrother, another Irish bookseller and printer, was not above publishing a miscellany of Swift's works at the same time, hoping to capitalize on the enthusiastic sale of the Irish edition. Faulkner in reaction to Fairbrother's piracy made the following statement when he published his eighteenmo edition: "This is the only genuine Collection of this Gentleman's Works that ever was publish'd excepting that which was done by Subscription in four Volumes octavo printed on very fine Genoa Paper, yet one Fairbrother hath in a Manner unprecedented publish'd a Medley in three Volumes, to which he hath had the Modesty to prefix this Gentleman's Name although without his (Knowledge) or Consent: besides the pieces that he hath printed of this supposed Author's, have whole Lines, Sentences and Paragraphs left out. . . . Besides this Edition doth not contain *Gulliver's Travels* nor the *Drapier's Letters*."[45]

No one can be certain whether George Faulkner wrote the following doggerel or whether some friend sent it to him for publication. Nonetheless, the writer was correct: Faulkner's fortune was made.

To the Author of the Dublin Journal

Poor, Honest George, Swift's Works to print,
Thy Fortune's made or nothing in't.
Subscribers, a vast number flew
There's no want of Money new.
The Dean's so great a Man of Taste,
All covet to read him in Haste.
More from thy Press than from any other;
Let what will happen to Fairbrother.[46]

Swift's friendship brought with it prosperity, but it also brought danger. Faulkner, unmindful of his last experience with possibly libelous material, printed a pamphlet titled *A New Proposal for the Better Regulation and Improvement of Quadrille.* The pamphlet, recommended to Faulkner by Swift, was the work of Josiah Hort, Bishop of Kilmore, and satirized the legal ability of Richard Bettesworth, sergeant-at-law and member of the Irish House of Commons. Again, George Faulkner was arrested for civil libel and for offending the public peace.[47] Bettesworth had Faulkner arrested on 3 March 1736 and brought before the House. The members found him guilty as charged and remanded him to Dublin's Newgate Prison. Faulkner petitioned for release on 5 March because he was "in a very bad state of health." Four days later he left Newgate in custody of the sergeant-at-arms of the House. Having begged pardon from the members of the Commons, he paid his court fines in copies of his new edition of Swift's works.[48] Jonathan Swift wrote an angry letter to Bishop Hort concerning Faulkner's imprisonment and demanded that Hort give monetary help to "the poor printer, who suffered so much upon your Lordship's account, confined to a dungeon among common thieves, and others with infectious diseases, to the hazard of his life; besides the expense of above twenty-five pounds, and besides the ignominy to be sent to Newgate like a common male-factor."[49]

Faulkner's prosecutions by the government made him a popular man among the anti-Whig faction. Freedom of the press, Dean Swift, and George Faulkner were the general topics of discussion in urban coffeehouses and taverns. Another heated topic of discussion concerned the right of Irish printers to send their books to England in competition with English printers and booksellers. Soon after Faulkner brought out his four volumes of Swift's *Works*, Benjamin Motte sued Faulkner in a London Chancery Court. The charge was infringement on the 1710 copyright law which protected Motte's right to print certain works of Swift in England. Faulkner's lawyer fought the case, contending that many of the pieces printed by Faulkner were not covered by the 1710 copyright law. Nevertheless, Lord Talbot granted Motte in November 1735 an injunction against Faulkner's shipping any Swift miscellanies into England. Faulkner tried to fight the injunction, but he found the court bias in favor of English booksellers too strong to overcome.[50]

Dean Swift took exception to Motte's legal action even though he wished to have his major works published in England. Motte's suit was one more case of English repression of Irish trade. He complained:

I am not qualified to judge in the fact having heard but one Side; only one thing I know, that the cruel Oppressions of this Kingdom by England are not to be borne. You send what Books you please hither, and the Booksellers here can send nothing to you that is printed here. As this is absolute Oppression, if I were a Bookseller in this Town, I would use all the safe Means to reprint London Books and run them into any Town in England that I could because, whoever neither offends the Laws of God, or the Country he lives in, committeth no Sin. It was the Fault of you and the Booksellers, who printed anything supposed to be mine, that you did not agree with each other to print them together, if you thought they would sell to any advantage ... Mr. Faulkner hath dealt so fairly with me that I have a great opinion of his Honesty though I have never dealt with him as Printer or Bookseller.[51]

In spite of Swift's ambiguous attitude toward Faulkner's activities for an Irish edition of his works, Faulkner continued to print material in the *Dublin Journal* sent him by Swift.

One such item concerned a new shipment of copper pence sent to Ireland in March 1737 to provide change for commodities bought with silver and gold coin (which were in short supply). The circumstances are unclear, but one might see it in this way: Swift, commenting ironically, said he might change some of the copper coin for gold. Faulkner misunderstood the statement and printed it for truth. In consequence to this publication Faulkner was arrested and brought before the authorities. Swift told Lord Oxford that Faulkner was "terribly abused, but not sent to prison, only left to Common Law for publishing a Libel; for so they called his paragraph."[52]

By 1740 George Faulkner's press had printed collected works by both Swift and Alexander Pope. In that year Pope, circuitous as always in handling his own writings, involved Faulkner in what Pope hoped would be a clandestine printing of the Swift-Pope letters. A package from an anonymous sender in Bath containing printed but unbound sheets of Pope-Swift letters arrived at Swift's deanery. Faulkner asked the authors for permission to publish the letters. Swift agreed, but Pope refused. Having printed three sheets before he received Pope's refusal, Faulkner stopped printing the edition. In reality Faulkner's compliance defeated Pope's plan to disavow an Irish edition as a piracy and still use the edition as copy for his own definitive edition, a plan which Pope had worked on printer-publisher Edmund Curll in 1735. Pope relented in January 1741 and gave Faulkner permission to publish, but Faulkner's edition appeared two months after Pope's on 20 June 1741.[53]

In January 1742 George Faulkner began the most ambitious printing project yet attempted in Ireland. Two hundred subscribers pledged eight guineas a person for a printing of the *Universal History from the Earliest Account of Time to the Present* in eight volumes folio.[54] Faulkner had proceeded beyond the third volume when he received word that a group of "itinerant projectors" intended to pirate his *Universal History* in octavo. The projectors were not members of the Dublin printing establishment. In consequence, a group of Dublin booksellers came to Faulkner's aid. This group, headed by George and Alexander Ewing, promised to help Faulkner fight the "pirates" if he would give them shares in a twenty-volume octavo edition, which Faulkner had not originally planned to publish—but consequently was forced to do so. This help from an unexpected quarter enabled Faulkner and the booksellers to rid themselves of the unwanted competition. This octavo edition in twenty volumes appeared for sale on 20 May 1746. His folio edition was advertised for sale shortly before Lord Chesterfield's arrival in September 1745.[55]

After 1741 Faulkner had no close contact with his patron, Dean Swift, or with Alexander Pope. Yet he continued to print editions of both their works. Pope was ill, and Swift's health was failing. Faulkner duly noted Pope's death on 6 June 1744 with the following short obituary: "On Wednesday Night late dyed at Twickenham, after a lingering Illness, Alexander Pope, whose writings best speak his Character."[56]

Jonathan Swift died sixteen months later on 19 October 1745. Faulkner bade his friend and patron farewell with the following obituary:

Last Saturday at 3:00 o'clock in the Afternoon dyed that great and eminent Patriot, the Reverend Dr. Jonathan Swift, Dean of St. Patrick's Dublin, in the 78th Year of his Age who was born in the Parish of St. Warburg's Dublin, the 30th of November 1667, at his Uncle Counsellor Godwin Swift's House in Hoey's Alley, which in those Times was the general Residence of the chief Lawyers. His Genius, Learning and Charity are so universally admired that for a Newswriter to attempt his Character would be the highest Presumption. Yet as the Printer hereof is proud to acknowledge his infinite Obligations to that Prodigy of Wit, he can only lament, that he is by no means equal to so bold an undertaking.
The Dean hath bequeathed the Bulk of his Fortune which is about 12000 £ to build and endow an Hospital for Lunaticks and Incurables, which said Hospital is to be called St. Patrick's, and to be erected near Stevens's. Dr. Sterne, late Bishop of Clogher left 600 £ towards the carrying on the said Hospital and William Coningham, Esq. 300 £.[57]

A month before Swift's death a group of the merchants of Dublin met at Dublin Castle to welcome Lord Chesterfield, the new Lord Lieutenant. George Faulkner, no doubt, was a member of that group. His friendship with Philip Dormer Stanhope, Earl of Chesterfield, began at this time; their correspondence covered the twenty-eight year period from Chesterfield's departure from Ireland in 1746 until his death in 1773.[58]

Chesterfield admitted readily that Faulkner's help made him both a popular regent and a just one. He conceded this point in a letter to Faulkner which read, "From my Time down to the Present, you have been in Possession of governing the Governors of Ireland, whenever you have thought to meddle with Business, and if you had meddled more with some, it might perhaps have been better for them and better for Ireland."[59]

In another letter Chesterfield compared Faulkner to Cicero's friend Titus Pomponius Atticus: "The celebrated Atticus seems to me to have been your prototype: he kept well with all parties, so do you; he was trusted and consulted by individuals on all sides, and so are you; he wrote some histories, so have you; he was the most eminent bookseller of the age he lived in; and he died immensely rich, and so will you. It is true he was a knight and you are not, but that you know is your own fault; and he was an Epicurean, and you are a Stoic."[60]

Chesterfield's allusion to a knighthood for George Faulkner shows the regard in which he held the printer. The Earl of Orrery was unsure at this time whether Faulkner received the knighthood, yet he was aware of the possibility of such a reward for the printer. Orrery had rejected the offer of books from a London friend and said, "We have them constantly reprinted in Dublin, and my Friend Sir George Faulkner (for he either is or should be a knight) sends them to me with perusals of various pieces before the public receives that satisfaction." In early 1747 a poem titled *Chivalrie No trifle or the Knight and His Lady: A Tale* described the imaginary moment when Faulkner and his wife were to become Sir George and Lady Faulkner. She thought about a new carriage to go with her new honor while her husband took a nap. Faulkner argued that the expense of maintaining

such a station was prohibitive. However, his wife was unmoved and the poem ended:

Prythee tell us the whole, how the supper was spoiled
How Arbuckle look'd pale–how Sir George near went wild!
How he wrote to Phil. Stanhope his word to make right good;
And send him immediately orders for knighthood.
How the letter was seal'd; when the letter was carry'd
How the knight often curs'd the sad day he was marry'd.
How impatient my lady still waits the reply;
For a lady she swears she must live! and will die.[61]

Although many people such as the Earl of Orrery spoke
of a knighthood for George Faulkner, there is no evidence
to prove that he received it. One can only speculate on Chesterfield's remark that Faulkner did refuse such an offer or
that the offer was never made because of political reasons.
The only times Faulkner was addressed as "Sir George" was
by political opponents or jealous place-seekers.

After Chesterfield left Ireland, Faulkner tried to render
his country the same impartial service he had rendered Chesterfield. In a city where tempers flared over politics, religion, and business ethics, Faulkner tried to remain an honest
and impartial observer in the midst of the tumult. One of his
lesser indiscretions which caused the Dubliners to castigate
him as a "Midas" was his printing of Lord Orrery's ill-
tempered book *Remarks on the Life and Writings of Dr.
Jonathan Swift, D.S.P.D.* Mary Granville Delany wrote to
her friend Mrs. Dewes:

The following epigram is now handed about on Lord Orrery's
Remarks on Swift:
  A sore disease this scribbling [itch] is
  His Lordship on his Pliny vain,
  Turns Madam Pilkington in [stitches],
  And now attacks the Irish Dean.
  Libel his friends when laid in ground?
  Pray good Sir you may spare your hints,
  His parallel I'm sure is found,
  For what he writes, George Faulkner prints.
  Had Swift provoked to this behaviour,
  Sure after death resentment cools,

And his last act bespoke their favour,
He founded a hospital for fools.[62]

Printing and politics always took a nationalistic turn. Since the beginning of the eighteenth century Irish printers had reprinted English books with or without permission. Because of a flaw in English law which saw Ireland as a separate but dependent kingdom, the copyright acts of 1710 and 1737 did not apply to Ireland. Most Irish booksellers agreed with Jonathan Swift's sentiment that, "If I were a Bookseller in this Town, I would use all Safe Means to reprint London Books and run them into any Town in England that I could." George Faulkner was luckier than other printers in having William Bowyer as his London contact. Nevertheless he was very vulnerable to acts of piracy by his fellow printers who could obtain stolen sheets from most London printing houses. Faulkner and Bowyer kept secret any transference of copy between London and Dublin in order to keep both English and Irish booksellers from stealing their property and printing it cheaply and shabbily.[63] Because of his large printing operations Faulkner was continually losing copy to Irish pirates who thought nothing of stealing from him. An example of such men were the Exshaw family, Richard Saunders, and Peter Wilson.

In spite of these precautions many London printers and booksellers had trouble with Irish "rapparees." Samuel Richardson, author and printer, charged that two of the three novels that he wrote, printed, and sent to Ireland found their way into a competitor's hands without copyright fees being paid to him. George Faulkner was Samuel Richardson's business associate for two of the three novels Richardson wrote. Therein lies a story which helped unjustly to lower the English opinion of George Faulkner.

On 14 February 1741 Faulkner and George Ewing advertised for sale *Pamela, or Virtue Rewarded*.[64] Faulkner's association with such an illustrious man gained him nothing but an infamous name from the English people and financial loss and much frustration from his Irish colleagues. When Faulkner published the Irish edition of *Pamela* he advertised two printings in two months, which would seem to indicate a great popularity of the book.[65]

When Richardson published his second novel, *Clarissa*, he contracted for Faulkner to have the Irish rights for a copy price of seventy guineas. The two booksellers haggled over the sum and Richardson claimed later that Faulkner paid him the seventy only after hard bargaining.[66]

When Richardson published his third novel, *Sir Charles Grandison*, he again contracted with Faulkner for the Irish printing rights. Unfortunately Richardson slowed the reprint process by first demanding that Faulkner agree to the following stipulations: 1) that the edition be limited to Ireland; 2) that Faulkner not advertise publication until Richardson gave him word to do so; 3) that Faulkner publish only two volumes at a time. Both men knew that there were many journeymen in London who would steal galley proofs and send them to Dublin, Paris, or Edinburgh, but Richardson chose to ignore the fact. Of course, the inevitable happened. Faulkner wrote Richardson on 4 August 1753 that three Dublin printers and one bookseller had posted their intentions to publish an edition of *Sir Charles Grandison*. While Faulkner waited for Richardson to send him more than four sheets, the "pirate" Peter Wilson had completed the first two volumes octavo, while Edward Exshaw and Richard Saunders had completed the same number in duodecimo.[67] Realizing there could be no profit in such a venture, Faulkner took his loss and stopped publication of this work. The extent of Faulkner's monetary losses in this affair is unknown. Although *Grandison* was not as popular a novel as *Pamela* the price on the book may have been the same as the price of *Pamela*—seventy guineas. Neither the Bradshaw collection at Cambridge nor the *Dublin Journal* for this period disclose any attempt by Faulkner to publish an edition of *Grandison*. Faulkner, realizing that his reputation as a businessman was at stake in London because of Richardson's printed accusations in a pamphlet, *Mr. Richardson's Case*, which was handed out gratis to Londoners, he wrote to the arbiter of London literary society, Dr. Samuel Johnson, who was both his friend and Richardson's friend. The letters are not extant; however, a reference to such a letter was made by Johnson in a letter to Richardson.[68] Subsequently, Richardson not only accused Faulkner of being the silent partner in this piracy action but also reprimanded him for sending "this strange, this inconsistent, this misrepresenting Letter of yours" to Samuel Johnson.[69]

All Irish printers viewed this argument as a national dispute; but Richardson was quick to deny this and say "this is not a contention between the booksellers of England and Ireland, and on doubtful property, but between a lawful proprietor of a new and moral work and . . . Messieurs Wilson, Exshaw and Saunders."[70] Faulkner, because of Richardson's accusation, was judged guilty by association and lost both money and reputation. Modern literary historians have unjustly lumped him with the Irish "rapparees" without even bothering to look beyond Samuel Richardson's pious outcries.

Faulkner's middle position in international business feuds placed him in danger of losing his reputation for honesty; his moderate position in national politics placed him in danger of losing his printing plant or, even worse, in danger of bodily harm. He tried to bring members of both political and religious factions together for dinners and conversation at his home in Essex Street. An anonymous friend, perhaps Dr. William Dunkin, recorded in poetic fashion, a scene at the Faulkner house where the host neither

> spares his mellow wine, nor dishes rare,
> But big of genius, and capacious heart,
> He pours his treasures eatable on board,
> And boon provokes his modest mates to pluck
> The present favours of the bounteous Gods,
> To celebrate glad carnivals, dissolve
> The frozen obstacles of anxious life,
> And heavy cares commit to the sceptered heads.[71]

However happy a picture this might present, Faulkner found himself in the unenviable middle position between two rabid political groups, the Court party and the Patriot party. Because of his friendship with a former Lord Lieutenant

(Chesterfield) Faulkner was accused of being a Court partisan by James Fitzgerald, Twentieth Earl of Kildare. Kildare, leader of the Patriot party, fought against the English or Court party, led by George Stone, Primate of Ireland, and Lionel Sackville, Duke of Dorset. As a result of English repression, Kildare took a memorial of Irish wrongs to King George II and asked for the recall of Dorset. The king recalled Dorset before the next Parliament, but not before Dorset established the right of English prerogative over Irish privilege. Patriot members organized themselves into a party after roll call defeats in 1749 and 1751 over disposal of the Irish money surplus. The English interest felt that the surplus should be allocated to the king as additional income; the Patriots felt that the money should be used to pay off the national debt.[72] In 1749 and 1751 the Court party triumphed. In 1753, however, the Patriot party triumphed by four votes on the measure. The Irish Parliament then sent the bill to the Lord Lieutenant who in turn sent it to the English Privy Council. The Council altered the bill and the Parliament again defeated it. The four men who cast decisive votes against the measure lost their government sinecures. Furthermore, the Duke of Dorset prorogued the Parliament on 31 January 1754.[73] Animosity toward the Duke grew higher. At the peak of anger against the Duke, George Faulkner made two grievous errors; while describing two meetings in two paragraphs in his *Journal* of 16 February, he recorded toasts drunk by the participants to the king and the Royal family. No one knows whether from negligence or from design, Faulkner added the health of the Duke of Dorset as a toast drunk by the Earl of Kildare and Speaker of the House, Henry Boyle. He also forgot to record the toast to "the glorious Memory of King William."[74] In reply to this slip the Patriots nicknamed Faulkner "Sir Tady Faulkner, printer in petto to the Court Party."[75] Political name-calling hurt Faulkner not at all; it was the threat of physical violence that frightened him. Dr. Barry, later Sir Edward Barry, president of the King's and Queen's College of Physicians, described in a letter to the Earl of Orrery Faulkner's confrontation with his wrathful tormentors:

George Faulkner published in his Journal the same day a list of the Ulster Toasts and inserted the Duke of D--'s health which was not drank, and omitted the glorious memory of King William's, two great faults. On Saturday Lord Kildare, Lord Carrick, and Mr. Creighton went to Faulkner's Shop, Lord Kildare charged him severely for daring to insert Falsehoods with his name, and tho' he narrowly then escaped punishment, solemnly threatened he would break what bones he had left in his body, if he did not in his next paragraph retract his Error and publish that the D. of D's health was not drank. . . . Some gentlemen who went into Faulkner's soon after, asked him what he would have done had Ld. Kildare struck him? He said he would not have received a blow from any man living without returning it, and that he would take the Law of him afterwards, and that during the whole Conversation he preserved a firmness and presence of Mind. His wife said that he had no business to strike any Lord, nor should not do it; that he was greatly frightened and that he had still a trembling on him; and she would not suffer any of them to come near him again, but engage them herself; and a Gentleman told me he saw Ld. Kildare there in a Chariot the second time that day, and Mrs. Faulkner talking to him red as a Turkey Cock, but she would not produce her husband. Faulkner was a considerable time with the Duke last night in great Consternation and Terror on many Accounts, but determined not to reprint anything to the [dis]honour[76] of his Grace.[77]

Lord Chesterfield expressed from London a well-bred contempt for Lord Kildare's treatment of Faulkner. He asked Major John (later General Sir John) Irwin the rhetorical question:

Who can think himself safe when gravity of deportment, dignity of character, candour, and impartiality, and even a wooden leg are no longer a protection? This rough manner of treating a man of letters, which my friend must be allowed to be, implies more zeal than knowledge; at least I never met with it among the canons of criticism. If my friend discovered some degree of human weakness, his other half at least showed the undaunted spirit of a Roman wife. Why is she not Lady Faulkner? And why are they not blessed with numerous issue, the happy compound of their father's stoicism and their mother's heroism?[78]

Faulkner mentioned nothing of his ordeal in his paper except a list of rhetorical questions about his loyalty and veracity:

Hath not he always had in View the Honour and Interest of Ireland?

Hath he ever infringed upon the Liberty or Property of any Persons whatever, either in his own Profession, or not of it?

Hath he ever printed in Public or Private, one single Paragraph to the Prejudice, Disreputation or Loss of any Person whatever?

Did he ever foment party Division or Dispute? On the Contrary, hath he not been as impartial a Newsprinter as ever published a Paper?

Hath he not printed such Paragraphs and Advertisements in his Journal, for all Persons whatever, that could be consistent with Law and Decency?

Whom hath he ever offended in Word, Thought, Deed, Writing, or Printing?

Whenever he was imposed upon by false Paragraphs (which have happened seldomer in his Paper than any in Europe of the same Standing) hath he not upon proper Application, always retracted them, or taken them out to the entire Satisfaction of the offended Persons and the Publick?

These Queries it is hoped, will satisfie the World, that he hath been a good Subject, an useful Member in Society, humane to his Fellow Creatures, and a Friend to his Country.[79]

Faulkner's suffering continued the following year when he lost his wife. She died 10 January 1755 after a "painful and lingering illness."[80] The loss of his wife, like the loss of his leg so many years before, was a painful experience; yet, it seemed to release some inner resource. He began traveling more and corresponding with more people. His name first appeared in 1756 on the rolls of the Dublin Society as a member. As a friend of the Society, Faulkner had printed agricultural hints from various members of the Society in his *Journal* as early as 8 January 1736/37.[81]

Faulkner corresponded at this time with Lord Chesterfield, Samuel Derrick, Charles O'Conor of Belanagare, William Bowyer, and no doubt with Samuel Johnson (although no letters are extant). He spent the winter of 1756 in England visiting Lord Chesterfield and his other friends. Chesterfield tells his friend Richard Chenevix, Bishop of Waterford, "My Friend George Faulkner dined with me here one day and I found him as sleek, as serene, and as serious as ever. He tells me that reading is not yet come in fashion in Ireland, and that more bottles are bought in one week than books in a year."[82]

When Faulkner returned to Dublin in the spring of 1757, he contacted Charles O'Conor of Belanagare concerning a religious-political proposal. O'Conor, a Roman Catholic landowner from County Roscommon, was a pamphleteer and member of the Catholic party. He and Faulkner, a Protestant, hoped to gain Samuel Johnson's help in writing an unspecified number of pamphlets in favor of Catholic enfranchisement. It would seem that Faulkner enclosed a letter to Johnson from Charles O'Conor offering him fifty guineas to write these pamphlets.[83] There are no letters extant between Faulkner and Johnson to indicate Johnson's reply.

Another trip to London in the fall of 1760 was perhaps a busman's holiday.[84] Faulkner definitely had plans for adding volumes to his *Works* of Swift. A year later (6 October 1761) he advertised in his *Journal* that a new edition of Swift's *Works* in eighteenmo was almost complete, "ten volumes are finished and the last is now in the Press and will be printed with all expedition."[85] Faulkner explained the slowness of publication as a result of finding "several original Sermons, Poems, Letters, which put the Editor under the Necessity of going twice to England for some of these Originals."[86] Even with his addition of new material to the *Works*, Faulkner did not officially advertise for sale this eighteenmo edition until 13 July 1762. Many times Faulkner had little material with which to make a salable book when he advertised. Consequently long periods of time passed between the time he advertised proposals for a book and the time he advertised it for sale. This period he used to add more Swift material.[87]

Soon a new threat appeared to jar Faulkner's well-ordered life. His friend Lord Chesterfield warned him that "Mr. Foote, who if I mistake not, was one of your *Symposion* while you was in London, and if so, the worse man he, takes you off as it is vulgarly called, that is, acts you in his new farce called the Orators. Since the government here cannot properly take notice of it, would it be amiss that you should show some spirit upon this occasion, either by way of stricture, contempt, or by bringing an action against him. I do not mean for writing the said farce but for acting it."[88]

Chesterfield felt that the acting out of the character Peter Paragraph was a libel against Faulkner's person. Faulkner's slowness in prosecuting Samuel Foote cannot be laid to his not having read the play. If Chesterfield had not sent him a copy of the play, his contacts in London, such as William Bowyer, would have. Foote originally had planned to satirize in his farce Thomas Sheridan's oratorical lectures, Samuel Johnson's involvement with the Cock-Lane ghost, and finally, the Robin Hood Debating Society.[89] When Johnson threatened to cane Foote if he "took him off," Foote of course looked elsewhere for a butt for his wit.[90] He did not have far to look. Foote's friend, "that little hopping fellow, the Dublin Journal man," was a logical choice.[91] Because the London dilettantes knew George Faulkner and his comical-pompous ways, Foote drew Faulkner as a caricature, a stage Irishman. Faulkner spoke with a lisp caused by missing teeth lost in a fall from a horse. His wooden leg also characterized him. Such obvious material gave Samuel Foote a chance to hobble about the stage lisping his answers in a broad Irish brogue. Peter Paragraph was a witness for the court investigation of Fanny, the Cock-Lane ghost. In the following dialogue Foote mimicked lines about Lord Chesterfield, the "peer" known by Faulkner:

Counsellor: Pray, Mr. Paragraph where was you born?

Paragraph: Sir, I am a native of Ireland, and born and bred in the city of Dublin.

Counsellor: When did you arrive in the city of London?

Paragraph: About the last Autumnal Equinox and now I recollect, my *Journal* makes a mention of my departure in the Bessborough Packet, Friday, October tenth, N.S. or stile.

Counsellor: Oh, then the *Journal* is yours?

Paragraph: Please, your worship, it is; and relating thereto I believe I can give you a pleasant conceit—Last week I went to visit a *peer*, for I know *peers*, and *peers* know me; quoth his lordship to me, Mr. Paragraph, with respect to your *Journal*, I would wish that your paper was whiter, or your ink blacker; quoth I to the peer, by way of reply, I hope you will own there is enough for the money; his lordship was pleased to laugh, it was such a pretty repartee, he he, he.[92]

Foote's comment on the "whiteness" of the paper and the "blackness" of the ink appears twice in the Chesterfield-Faulkner correspondence and appears to be a comfortable old joke between the two.[93] Foote probably learned of this joke from Faulkner.

Contrary to Chesterfield's exhortations, Faulkner did not institute libel proceedings against Samuel Foote during the London run of the play. The farce closed quietly on September 14, when Foote's summer patent at the Little Haymarket expired for that year. Foote then brought his play to Dublin, arriving approximately the first week of October 1762. When *The Orators* opened at Smock Alley, Faulkner gave his employees tickets to it so that they might hiss Foote from the stage. Meanwhile Faulkner secreted himself in a remote part of the theater and waited for the success of his scheme. Unfortunately for him, the audience liked the burlesque of Faulkner in act one. On the following day, his employees told him they were so pleased to see their employer on the stage that they had no heart to hiss him. Furthermore, Faulkner's Dublin friends rallied him so unbearably that he could not stand in the doorway of his shop without becoming a figure of derision.[94] Exasperated by this treatment, Faulkner finally sued Foote for libel; the trial took place at the Four Courts in Dublin with Judge Christopher Robinson of the King's Bench presiding. The judge decided in favor of Faulkner, and Foote "suddenly quit that Metropolis, and returned to England, leaving his bail to pay the penalty of his bonds, who notwithstanding the reports to the contrary, he afterwards reimbursed."[95]

When Foote returned to England he decided to pen a farcical answer to Faulkner titled *The Trial of Samuel Foote for a Libel on Peter Paragraph*. He gained the last word by declaiming Faulkner-Paragraph to be equally guilty, since "if my client is a libellor for writing the Orators, Peter Paragraph for printing it is as guilty every whit."[96] Tate Wilkinson, Samuel Foote's fellow actor added the footnote that "it is whimsical truth that Mr. George Faulkner actually printed, published and sold the Orators."[97] There is no other corroboration of Wilkinson's claim that Faulkner reprinted Foote's "The Orators"; yet such a turnabout would fit Faulkner's sense of humor as well as his sense of justice.

Faulkner's sense of humor, rather than his ethical conduct, took control of the printer in this episode. However, it is one of the times in which he allowed his sense of humor to outweigh his sense of honor in illegally publishing the pamphlet. Lord Chesterfield thought Faulkner was fully justified in any action he took against Samuel Foote. When Foote lost a leg as a result of a fall from a horse, Lord Chesterfield commented smugly to Faulkner, "I can not help observing with some satisfaction that Heaven has avenged your cause, as well and still more severely than the courts of temporal justice in Ireland did, having punished your adversary Foote in the part offending."[98]

During the run of the play, Faulkner was busy with his lifelong project of making available to the public as complete a collection of Swift's works as he could assemble. Before his argument with Samuel Foote, Faulkner planned to write a new preface to his proposed eleven-volume edition in octavo, hoping to justify to the public the inclusion of letters from Jonathan Swift to himself. He also wished to defend himself against the attacks of John Hawkesworth, editor since 1755 of the London editions of Swift's works.[99]

Hawkesworth disputed Faulkner's claim that Swift helped edit the first six volumes of the *Works*. Angered by Hawkesworth's attack, George Faulkner made the following declaration in his new preface to the 1763 edition. He hoped the inclusion of the Swift-Faulkner letters "will convince the World of the Intimacy the Author was pleased to favour the Printer with, he hopeth he may escape Censure; these Letters being now first printed, to satisfy the Reader that Mr. Faulkner was not only the Dean's Publisher, but favoured with his Friendship, and consulted by him on many Occasions, to explain this, it is proper to inform the Curious that Dr. Hawksworth, a learned and ingenious Gentleman, who was imposed upon by some London Bookseller, wrote a Preface and a few very trifling Notes to an Edition of the foregoing Miscellanies."[100]

Faulkner's 1763 edition was a composite group of reissued volumes, except for a new volume eleven.[101] He advertised for sale in April 1763 his tenth and eleventh volumes of Swift's *Works*, as well as a past printing of *The Life of Edward Earl of Clarendon and His History of the Rebellion* in three volumes, octavo or one volume, folio. Faulkner, now living and working on the Blind Quay, kept busy turning out books by important English writers, such as William Shenstone's *Works in Verse and Prose* and William Warburton's edition of the *Works of Alexander Pope* in nine volumes, small octavo.[102]

After the first week of June 1765, at approximately the same time that he advertised two more volumes of Swift's *Works* (the twelfth and thirteenth volumes), Faulkner moved his printing shop-home from Blind Quay to 15 Parliament Street.[103] Faulkner's haste for a new home, as well as his preoccupation with his printing business, was the reason for a humorous incident with which Faulkner, no doubt, later regaled his dinner guests. Robert Jephson, parodying Faulkner's rambling and often disconnected manner of writing, tells of the incident in the way Faulkner might have told it to dinner guests:

It may be worthwhile to mention a very entertaining anecdote (for the satisfaction of the curious) relating thereunto: When my House was building, I happened to be out of the way, penning an advertisement for an agreeable companion to pay half the expense of a post chaise, to see that stupendous curiosity of nature, the Giant's Causeway, about which 'tis still a doubt amongst the learned whether it be done in the common way by giants, or whether it be an effort of spontaneous nature, and my house was without any staircase; whereby the upper stories were rendered useless, unless by the communication of a ladder placed in the street. But considering my misfortune in wanting my member, and the carelessness of hackney coachmen, who drive furiously through the streets at all hours, in a state of drunkenness from spiritous liquors, whereby the ladder might be shook or thrown down when I was ascending it, I thought it better to rebuild my house, and it has at present a staircase by which there is convenient and elegant communication between all parts of said tenement—it is somewhat remarkable that my house in Essex-street had no staircase, whereby nature seemeth to point out, that having but one leg, I ought not to attempt climbing, and should remain on the ground floor.[104]

At this time, Faulkner was better able to entertain his guests at home. "If it be an Happiness," he wrote to Charles O'Conor, "I have that Pleasure of being visited by most Foreigners who come hither; and how can I help shewing them the Civilities of my Table at which People of all Religions and Countries are welcome." Faulkner was true to his sentiments. Frederick Augustus Hervey, Anglican Bishop of Cloyne, visited the Faulkner home, as did Dr. Patrick Fitzsimmons, Roman Catholic Archbishop of Dublin.[105] In the next ten years George Faulkner entertained two Lord Lieutenants of Ireland, Lord Townshend and Earl Harcourt.[106] He was a considerate host; for instance, he described in a letter to Charles O'Conor how he handled the presence of Lord Townshend at one of his dinners: "I never invite any of my Friends on these Occasions; but request his Excellency to invite his own Friends to fill the Table."[107]

One guest, Richard Cumberland, Ulster secretary under Lord Halifax and author of the play *The West Indian*, described a night at Faulkner's:

He gave good meat and excellent claret in abundance; I sate at his table once from dinner till two in the morning whilst George swallowed immense potations with one solitary, sodden strawberry at the bottom of his glass which he said was recommended to him by his doctor for its cooling properties. He never lost his recollection or equilibrium the whole time and was in excellent foolery; it was a singular coincidence, that there was a person in company, who had received his reprieve at the gallows, and the very judge, who had passed sentence of death upon him. This did not in the least disturb the harmony of the society, nor embarrass any human creature present. All went off perfectly smooth and George adverting to an original portrait of Dean Swift, which hung in his room, told us abundance of excellent and interesting anecdotes of the Dean and himself with minute precision and an importance irresistibly ludicrous. There was also a portrait of his late lady, Mrs. Faulkner, which either made the painter or George a liar, for it was frightfully ugly, whilst he swore she was the most divine object in creation. . . . In process of time he became an alderman; I paid my court to him in that character, but I thought he was rather marred than mended by his dignity. George grew grave and sentimental, and gravity sate as ill upon George as a gown and square cap would upon a monkey.[108]

In July 1767 Faulkner's fellow Dubliners elected him to the post of high sheriff. Nevertheless, Faulkner, plagued by chronic ill health and devoted to the completion of his Swift collection, resigned his high position with the following notice in his *Journal:*

Dublin, July 28

To the Right Hon. Lord Mayor, Aldermen, Sheriffs, Commons, and Citizens of the City of Dublin

My Lords and Gentlemen,

I can not sufficiently express my grateful Acknowledgements to your Lordship, and my worthy Fellow-Citizens, for the great Honour you were pleased to confer on me by electing me into the respectable Office of High Sheriff of this very great and trading City, which I have always endeavoured to serve to the utmost of my Abilities, but, as my present state of Health will not permit me to execute that honourable, but active and laborious Office, with Credit to myself, or Advantage to the Public, I hope your Lordship, the Aldermen, Sheriffs, Commons, and the rest of my worthy Fellow-Citizens, will be so indulgent as to excuse me on this Occasion. At the same Time be assured, that in every other Thing within my Sphere, it shall be my constant Study to promote the Welfare of my Country in general, and that, in particular, of this my native City. I am, my Lord, and Gentlemen, with greatest Respect, Honour and Esteem, your most grateful, much obliged, obedient humble Servant, and Fellow-Citizen.

George Faulkner[109]

Relieved of his official duties, Faulkner could return to his first love: publication of Swift's *Works.* His collection of volumes had grown from the seminal four volumes of 1735 to the eleven volumes of the 1763 octavo and eighteenmo editions. From 1763 to 1767 he added five more volumes. Three of the five volumes contained new letters obtained from the London edition.[110] In 1768 Faulkner added three more volumes and advertised a final twentieth volume in

1769.[111] However, he did not reissue his twenty volumes as a set until 1772.[112]

Besides his Swift editions, George Faulkner was busy pursuing another lifetime project: promotion of a history of Ireland. This interest in history in general and Irish history in particular appeared in his letters to Samuel Derrick and Charles O'Conor.[113] Faulkner's position as a publisher and newspaper editor helped him to popularize the idea of a history of Ireland. He advertised as early as 1737 the cheapness and availability of historical documents printed as a subscription venture:

Proposals to be printed for the printing by Subscription: Subsidia ad Historiam Hiberniae seu Foedera, Literae, Chartae, Regiae.

1. To publish in one Volume all the Letters and other publick Acts relating to the Affairs of Ireland in the Order of their Time, now dispensed in above 40 Volumes in Folio, the Purchase of which Books would fall very little short of one hundred Pounds.

2. Price to Subscribers, 30 shillings.

3. 300 Sheets in Folio.[114]

Notwithstanding the cheapness of such a book venture, few subscribers contacted Faulkner. The pages of the *Dublin Journal* contained no further mention of the project. Again Faulkner advertised for subscriptions for a history of Ireland by Henry Brooke, the playwright and pamphleteer. Besides advertising the proposal for printing, George Faulkner prefaced an article by Brooke for the front page of the *Dublin Journal*: "Since most Nations are fond of giving Accounts of the Antient State of their Countries; we think that the following Preface to a new History of Ireland by Henry Brooke, Esq. (for which Subscriptions are now being taken in) will be acceptable to all our readers."[115]

Henry Brooke thought about the idea for twenty years, but never published the history. Despite his several failures in inspiring an Irishman to write Irish history, Faulkner did help Charles O'Conor publish *Dissertations on the History of Ireland* in 1766. Both Faulkner and O'Conor were instrumental in giving vogue to Lord Lyttleton's *History of the Life of Henry the Second and the Age in which He Lived*. Since

Lord Lyttleton's histories included the invasion of Ireland, both O'Conor and Faulkner coaxed Dr. Thomas Leland of Trinity College, Dublin, into writing a *History of Ireland from the Time of Henry II.*[116]

When the Dublin Society formed an Antiquarian Committee "to enquire into the antient state of arts and literature and into the other antiquities of Ireland," Faulkner's *Dublin Journal* played an important role in disseminating the Committee's findings. One resolution of the second meeting of the Committee on 18 May 1772 was:

Resolved, That the appointment of this committee be notified to the publick in an advertisement in the Dublin Journal, and that a request of the committee be made in said advertisement, that such persons as are desirous and have it in their power to assist the committee in its national researches, and contribute to the national undertaking, will communicate the titles of such ancient Irish manuscripts as may be in their hands, and an account of such other material as they are possessed of, and which they think may be useful in forwarding the designs of the committee; directed to Dr. Chaigneau at the Dublin Society's House in Grafton-street.[117]

One of the first projects of the Committee was the purchase of the manuscript of a seventeenth-century work, *Oygygia*, by Roderick O'Flaherty for twenty guineas. The Committee, possibly through suggestions by both Dr. Leland and George Faulkner, appointed Faulkner's friend Charles O'Conor as editor. Faulkner advertised O'Conor's edition of the work in April 1775.[118]

Although Faulkner kept busy publishing books and editing his newspaper, his fellow Dubliners elected him alderman of the city of Dublin in 1770. His new dignity as alderman did not prevent his becoming involved in a paper feud with another alderman, Gorges Edmond Howard, lawyer, poet, dramatist, and essayist. On 22 May 1770 Faulkner printed in his *Journal* an advertisement for a new periodical, *The Monstrous Magazine*, published by George Ewing and containing "whatever tends to exhort amazement in art or nature, fact or fiction, occasionally interspersed with the impossible. Inscribed to the incomparable author of Almeyda or the Rival

Kings; as also the Tragedy of Tarah, and other literary productions, in hopes of his future favours."[119]

Alderman Howard felt Faulkner had abused him by printing the advertisement and sent him a stinging rebuke. Faulkner held the letter for a week and then printed it in his newspaper. Howard wrote: "Mr. Howard is little obliged to Mr. Faulkner, his old Acquaintance, and protested Friend, for inserting in his Paper, the nonsensical, impudent, Advertisement of that waspish impertinent Jackanapes Ewing—but what should Mr. Howard expect from the Publisher of Lord Orrery's Remarks on the Man who raised him and made him what he is. But Mr. Howard finds that Mr. Faulkner reverses St. Paul's Maxim, that Godliness is great Gain, for Mr. Faulkner great Gain is Godliness."[120]

This explosion by Howard triggered a hoax that amused Dublin for weeks. Robert Jephson, parliamentarian and playwright, took advantage of this one-sided argument to write epigrams about both Faulkner and Howard. He signed their names to the poems and sent copies to Hoey's *Mercury* and Faulkner's *Journal*. The culmination of the hoax was the publication of two mock heroic poems, supposedly written by the disputants.[121]

An Epistle to Gorges Edmond Howard, Esq. with Notes Explanatory, Critical and Historical by "George Faulkner" was the more popular of the two. This pamphlet, loaded with terms Faulkner had used for over forty years, parodied Faulkner's loose journalistic style. Jephson's imitation of Faulkner's style went through five printings in Dublin and one in London. The *Monthly Review* in London stated that the parody was "An excellent piece of humour, by which the reader who is acquainted with the character of Mr. Faulkner, the printer, will be highly entertained, at the expense of that gentleman."[122]

After Dublin had recovered from Jephson's witticism at Faulkner's and Howard's expense, George Faulkner was accorded a moderate amount of peace and contentment. He brought out a twenty volume reissue of Swift's *Works* in 1772; in 1773 he completed his printing for Lord Lyttleton's *History of King Henry the Second*. He also printed in 1773 and advertised for sale on 24 April for the bookseller Richard Moncrieffe the Irish edition of Dr. Leland's *History of Ireland from the Invasion of Henry II*. Eighteen months after George Faulkner's patron, Lord Chesterfield, died, Faulkner advertised for sale on 13 December 1774 three volumes of Chesterfield's *Works*.[123]

On 20 August 1775, Faulkner and some friends went to dine at a suburban tavern. Unfortunately the tavern had been recently painted, and Faulkner developed respiratory trouble. He then developed violent hiccups, followed by a retention of urine. His advanced age further weakened him. After an illness of nine days, he died on 30 August 1775.[125] Thomas Todd, who now adopted Faulkner's name, printed this short obituary: "Yesterday morning at six o'clock in the 76th year of his age, died Alderman George Faulkner, who was printer of this journal upwards of 50 years."[126]

Even in death George Faulkner would be near his patron Jonathan Swift. He was laid to rest in a burial ground called the "Cabbage Garden" at the foot of Cathedral Lane in what was then the parish of St. Patrick's. The following is a transcript from Faulkner's tombstone made by Richard Robert Madden in 1867:

> Here lieth the body of George Faulkner,
> Alderman of the City of Dublin
> who was a man of superior benevolence
> of mind and goodness of heart.
>
> He was esteemed by the Great which
> honour he never sought; and by the
> Poor, who were the constant objects
> of his munificence.
>
> His heart was ever open to the distressed,
> and his purse to the necessities of mankind.
> He was a sincere friend and a real patriot;
> but of no party or faction his country being
> the first object of his attachment. In the
> exercise of every filial, conjugal and social
> duty he was prominent. In fine, he earned the
> esteem of all the country – of none the hatred.
>
> He departed from his life the 30th of August
> 1775 in the 76th year of his age.[127]

The Letters of George Faulkner

GEORGE FAULKNER TO WILLIAM HOGARTH § The set of prints to which Faulkner refers can be identified from an advertisement in the *London Daily Post and General Advertiser* for 24 November 1740, announcing the impending publication of a print called "The Provoked Musician," a "companion to a print representing a Distressed Poet, published sometime since. To which will be added a third on painting to compleat the sett; but as this subject may turn upon an affair between the Right Honourable L--d M---r and the author, it may be retarded for sometime."[1] Actually the third print never appeared, and Faulkner's plan to act as importer necessarily fell through.

1. Ronald Paulson, *The Graphic Art of William Hogarth*, 1:184 ff.

George Faulkner to William Hogarth
(BM Add. Mss 27995)

Dublin, Nov. 15, 1740

Sir

I was favoured with a Letter from Mr. Delany[2] who tells me, that you are going to publish three Prints. Your Reputation here is sufficiently known to recommend anything of yours; and I shall be glad to serve you. The Duty on Prints is ten (P.) Cent in Ireland. You may send me 50 Setts, providing you will take back what I cannot sell. I desire no other Profit than what you allow in London to those who sell them again. I have often the Favour of drinking your Health with Dr. Swift, who is a great Admirer of yours, and hath made mention of you in his Poems with great Honour, and desired me to thank you for your kind Present, and to accept of his Service.[3]

I am Sir
Your Most Obedient, and Most
humble Serv't.
George Faulkner

2. Patrick Delany (1685–1768), Dean of Down.
3. Jonathan Swift, "The Legion Club," in *The Poems of Jonathan Swift*, 3:839.

GEORGE FAULKNER TO THE EARL OF ORRERY § This letter is important for its information concerning Faulkner's printing and selling of Orrery's ill-natured book on Jonathan Swift. Both London and Dublin audiences were amused by the book. A. Millar in London and George Faulkner in Dublin printed and sold editions of Lord Orrery's *Remarks on the Life and Writings of Dr. Jonathan Swift*. . . . For example the "Monthly Review," *Gentleman's Magazine* 22 (November 1751):107–23 and (December 1751): 475–87 titillated the appetites for scandal of the readers by printing excerpts from Orrery's book that concerned Swift's supposed marriage to Esther Johnson (415) and Swift's being the illegitimate son of Sir William Temple (415).

While Millar's edition created a demand because of the scandal in the book, Faulkner's edition caused a furor because of Faulkner's past close relationship with Jonathan Swift. Because George Faulkner owed so much of his success to the patronage of Swift, many people reasoned that he was sacrificing Swift's good name for financial gain. Dubliners such as Mary Granville Delany felt that the publication by Faulkner of such gossip was a desecration of Swift's memory. It seems that Faulkner's practical impulse won out over his moral impulse. As he noted in this letter he sold three hundred copies in a week, something seldom seen in eighteenth-century Dublin.

George Faulkner to the Earl of Orrery[1]
(Trinity College Library, Cambridge University)

Dublin, November 30. 1751

My Lord
The six Mails that arrived on Thursday honoured me with five Letters from your Lordship. I told you in my last that there was an amasing Demand for the Remarks which still continues. All the Judicious and Learned, as well as those that are unprejudiced, allow it to be the finest and best written Piece in the English Tongue. I think my Sale is not in-

ferior to Mr. Millar's,[2] having sold above 300 one Week, which is more than ever was known to be disposed of in so short a Time in Dublin. I am likely to be hanged, drawn and quartered for printing and publishing this Libel against my best Friend and Benefactor, and am charged on this Account with the utmost Ingratitude to the Dean; and my ill State of Health still confining me to my Chamber, some ignorant People have given out, that I dare not come into my Shop for Fear of being insulted or very ill used; but these Reports do not give me the least Uneasiness. I am well enough to see Company in my own Apartment, altho' I am not well enough to go into the Air, and those Persons who are Gentlemen of the best Taste and Learning in the Kingdom all agree, that your Lordship's Remarks are beyond any Work that they have seen; and here, my Lord, I must be very proud, for they all tell me, it is not only the best written, but the best printed Book that ever was done in Ireland. There is a loud Complaint against your Lordship from the Manager, the Musicians, the Vintners and Coffee Men, that this Week they have all been neglected on your Account; for instead of the Ladies and Gentlemen going to Plays, Balls, assemblies, Taverns and Coffee-Houses, they are all now taken up with reading the Earl of Orrery's Remarks on Dr. Swift's Life; and what is worse, more and more People are likely to read it, and to neglect all Diversions whatever: Even Cards are laid aside to read this bewitching Book; and the Ladies, (let their Numbers be ever so great) are silent and dumb as Mutes, to listen, and *catch with greedy Ear*. I am told there are to be several Thrusts and Shots made at me, in different Papers next Week; but, as I fight under your Lordship's Banner, I hope I shall be able to resist them. I thank your Lordship most heartily for the Letter you wrote to Wilson and Williamson from whom I have not heard lately, and suppose they have dropped their Design.[3] I did not publish until I had printed Dr. Barry's Alteration. I am extreamly glad your Lordship's Eyes are well; mine are most tormenting. I cannot recollect, that I ever omitted answering any one of your Lordship's Letters; but you know the Winds are very contrary this Time of Year. I believe I did once tell your Lordship, that as I could not sleep one Night, I got up early in the Morning, and began a Life of the Dean upon which I never proceeded further, not having Time or Capacity for such a Work; and indeed your Lordship's is so well executed, and in such universal Reputation, it will be Vain for any one else to attempt it, as immortal Fame will spread yours thro' the World, whilst any others must limp very slowly, even thro' this Kingdom. I never did think Mr. Bettenham[4] to blame, because I know him to be a Gentleman of unblemished and universal good Character; but there might be Sheets stolen from his Press, as well as there have been from mine, and from others in both Kingdoms. I am sorry this Affair hath given him so much Uneasiness, which I did not intend, but for his Service. I would write to him but that I can hardly see to finish this Letter, and beg he will accept of my best Wishes and Compliments. I am, my Lord, with most humble Respects to Lord and Mr. Boyle, your Lordship's most dutiful, most obed't. and most humble Serv't.

George Faulkner

1. Faulkner advertised for sale in his *Dublin Journal*, 19–23 November 1751, his edition of *Remarks on the Life and Writings of Dr. Jonathan Swift, D.S.P.D.* . . . "large Octavo printed on a fine Paper and a new Elzevir Type with a Profile of Dr. Jonathan Swift, D.S.P.D. from an original Picture painted by Mr. Barber, and engrav'd by Mr. Willison." The copies of this book that I have seen at Cornell, Yale and Indiana bear the date 1752. However, Donald Eddy of the Olin Library, Cornell, advised me that eighteenth-century books published in the last two months of the year took the date of the following year. William Cagle, assistant librarian of the Lilly Library, Indiana University, showed me the red leather-bound copy of the *Remarks* which Faulkner inscribed to Orrery as a presentation copy. Many Dubliners (Mary Granville Delany for one) criticized Faulkner's moral ethic in printing Orrery's book; see *The Autobiography and Correspondence of Mary Granville, Mrs. Delany*, 3:79. Teerink's *Bibliography of the Writings of Jonathan Swift*, pp. 415–16, mentions three pamphlets attacking Orrery and Faulkner because of the book: *A Candid Appeal from The Late Dean Swift to The Right Hon. Earl of O----y*, etc. (London: W. Owen, 1752); *A Letter to The Right Reverend Bishop of Clogher, etc.*, to which is added *A Letter to The Right Honourable, John, Earl of Orrery, Occasioned by the Character which His Lordship gives of Dean Swift's Sermon on the Trinity, in His Remarks on the Life and Writings of the Dean*, etc. (London: J. Noon, 1752); *A Letter from a Primate to a Pretender Found by a Patriot Standerby. To which is added The Oracle of Dagon. And A Letter from Dean Swift to*

George F---k--r (Isle of Man: Printed in the Poultry Yard by Benjamin Free for The Gaffmaker, 1752).

2. A. Millar was a publisher and bookseller who had the rights for the London edition. Teerink's *Bibliography of the Writings of Jonathan Swift*, p. 415, lists five editions in octavo and duodecimo and one edition by Faulkner in octavo and one in duodecimo. However, these printings must have been substantial.

3. Plomer et al, *Dictionary of Printers and Booksellers at Work in England, Scotland and Ireland, 1726–1775*, p. 426, states that both Peter Wilson and M. Williamson were booksellers or printers in Dublin at this time. "Their design" could refer to an attempt to pirate an edition of Orrery's *Remarks*. As mentioned previously, Faulkner was not so fortunate in stopping Peter Wilson two years later in 1753 when Wilson, Exshaw, and Saunders pirated Samuel Richardson's *Sir Charles Grandison* for an Irish edition.

4. There is no positive identification for "Mr. Bettenham." Perhaps he was one of a number of printers to whom Millar in London sent copies of Orrery's book, only to have them stolen by dishonest journeymen. They in turn sent the galley proofs to Scottish, Irish, or French printers.

GEORGE FAULKNER TO WILLIAM BOWYER § George Faulkner's association with William Bowyer, Jr., dated as early as 1722. Many of the pamphlets which Bowyer sent to Faulkner, Faulkner would, in turn, send to Lord Chesterfield and Lord Orrery. Faulkner's allusion to the "Bishop's Works" could possibly allude to an edition of Bishop Berkeley's tracts in a popular *Miscellany* which Faulkner had advertised the previous September as being "in the Press and speedily will be published."[1]

1. *Dublin Journal*, 13–17 November 1753, "This Day is published by the Printer hereof. Price bound 2s 8d halfpenny, stitched in blue paper 2s 2p." A *Miscellany Containing Several Tracts on Various Subjects* by the Bishop of Cloyne.

George Faulkner to William Bowyer
(The Hyde Collection)

Dublin, April 10. 1753

Dear Sir

I have many of your kind Favours to Answer; but have been very much indisposed of late, which prevented my writing to you to acknowledge your many Civilities to me, and particularly your last generous Present, which I am not entitled to, in any Shape whatever. What you got by the Bishop's Works was accidental: you might have lost more than you gained, and perhaps you may be a loser in other Pieces of which I have now two in my House which I will send you from the Press, to publish immediately after me. Your sending of pamphlets, etc. to me, are extreamly useful; for [crossed out] altho' I reprint very few of them, I have an opportunity of obliging many Friends, and particularly our Bishop,[2] who very often calls to see me, tells with Pleasure when he hears from you; and who, I can assure you, has the highest Regard and Esteem for you, and would be very glad to serve you. I am desired to enquire, what is the Price of Hebrew Hutchinson's Works I mean, the Gentleman whose Works were printed at your House, when I had the Favour of working with you.[3] If I have not fully answered your Letters, be pleased to let me know, as I cannot yet stir out of my Room to examine them. Mrs. Faulkner joins in best Wishes and Compliments to you, Mrs. Bowyer and your Son, with D. Sir, your much obliged Friend, and sincere, humble Serv't.

George Faulkner

You will oblige me by sending the enclosed letter to Mr. Lockart Davis.[4]

2. Faulkner could mean either the Archbishop of Dublin, Dr. Charles Cobb, or Faulkner's friend, Dr. Robert Clayton, Bishop of Clogher.

3. *British Museum General Catalogue of Printed Books*, 11:376, lists the following possibility which would coincide with Faulkner's stay with the Bowyers in London: *Moses's Principia of the Invisible Parts of Matter of Motion, of Visible Forms* . . . by J[ohn] H[utchinson] (London, 1724); the reference is vague.

4. Lockyer Davis, London bookseller who was a nephew of Charles Davis, one of the London publishers of Swift's *Works*. See Plomer et al, *Dictionary of Printers and Booksellers at Work in England, Scotland and Ireland, 1726–1775*, p. 72.

GEORGE FAULKNER to *** § This letter to the unidentified recipient would appear to be a business letter. Judging from the arrangements made for sending the printed but unbound books to Faulkner this would appear to be the usual arrangement for Bowyer to send books to Faulkner and vice versa. Other possibilities, however, could be Charles Reymer, the printer for Lockyer Davis, or Thomas Becket, who imported foreign books and had them translated from French and the ancient languages.

George Faulkner to ***

Dublin, Oct. 27, 1763

Sir

I am very sorry to tell you, that The Loves of Chaeres,[1] etc. are not yet come to Hand. Pray enquire who you sent them to in Chester, and in what Ship they put them on Board, and how they were directed to me, as I have had no account from any one about them but yourself. Although Williams's Ship got safe to Dublin, yet many Passengers were washed over Board, and many Parcels of Goods thrown into the Sea to lighten her, but, I hope the one you sent did not meet with that Fate. When these Books come to Hand I shall get them bound and delivered, as the most worthy and benevolent Mr. Lockman desires having the highest Regard and Esteem and his most agreeable and aimiable Family to all of whom be pleased to make my best Respects, which will oblige.[2]

Your most humble Serv't.

George Faulkner

I should write Mr. Lockman but that I am very much indisposed with a cold and inflamed Eyes.

1. *British Museum General Catalogue of Printed Books*, 5:452, gives the full title as *The Loves of Chaereas and Callirrhoe.* Written originally in Greek by Chariton of Aphrodisos, 2 vols. (London, T. Becket and P. DeHondt, 1764).

2. *Dublin Journal*, 26–29 November 1763. Faulkner advertised *The Loves of Chaereas and Callirrhoe* for sale on this date. Sometime in

November, after Faulkner had received the letter from his correspondent, the ship carrying the unbound books arrived. Given due time for binding, Faulkner was able to advertise the books ready for sale.

GEORGE FAULKNER TO LORD ORRERY § The following excerpt from George Faulkner to Lord Orrery is published for the first time. The Countess of Cork and Orrery, when she edited *The Orrery Papers*, omitted the paragraph concerning the bankrupting of the Dublin merchants. She used only two sentences, "Sheridan is undone. His Theatre in Smock Alley being torn to pieces in the inside, and he will appear no more, he says, upon the stage."[1] Esther Sheldon in her book, *Thomas Sheridan of Smock Alley*, pp. 199–205, covers this incident concisely and accurately.

1. *Orrery Papers*, 2:125.

George Faulkner to Lord Orrery
(Houghton Library MS English 218.5 Orrery Papers)

Dublin, March 12, 1754

It gives me great pain to tell your Lords. that I believe Ireland is at this time the most unhappy, miserable, distracted Country in Europe, as parties run higher now than ever was known, and credit and Trade sink lower than words can describe. Last Wednesday–Dillon and Farrele, two very eminent Bankers, failed for a very large Sum, which caused a great run upon our Banks, most or all of whom would be obliged to shut up, had it not been for our Government, and the Associations of our nobility, gentry, merchants and traders, who all agreed to take Bank notes in payment; notwithstanding we have daily Bankruptcies.[2] Caroline at the Phoenix Tavern in Castle Street broke last Sunday. One Lynch a Merchant yesterday,–and one Rich a Mercer, shut this morning. And,

44

if Bookselling doth not mend, I must quit business, go to London, and beg the honour of your Lordship's protection and favour, as nothing is read here but the most Scurrilous pamphlets and bitter Invectives. Sheridan is undone. His Theatre in Smock Alley being torn to pieces in the inside, and he will appear no more, he says, upon the Stage. What shall I do, whom have no Estate, am in the decline of Life, almost blind, want my Limbs, and am run with Rheumatic Pains. Yet I will not despair, as I trust in providence that I have some good friends, particularly my great, good, and worthy Benefactor and Patron, Lord Corke.

2. George Faulkner paints a gloomy picture of the Dublin bankruptcies. However, he reflects a happier picture in his *Dublin Journal*, 5–9 March 1754: "His Majesty's Letter of Credit is come over, for paying off the National Debt of this Kingdom, amounting to 76,000 £, the Circulation of which Sum in ready Cash at this critical Time must be the greatest Benefit and Advantage to this unhappy Nation, the Publick Credit of which is at a very low Ebb occasioned by our Folly in the Neglect of Tillage, and the vast Importation of all sorts of Grain, Spirits, Wine, and Manufactures."

GEORGE FAULKNER TO EDMUND BURKE § Dublin admitted few men to the "freedom of the City." Burke's position as secretary to the Marquess of Rockingham gave him respectability in the eyes of the citizens of Dublin. Faulkner's gossip about the trial of a peer for idiocy becomes both confusing and boring to the modern reader. Faulkner's account in his newspaper, the *Dublin Journal*, was more concise in stating that the "Earl of Ely is not an Idiot or of unsound Mind."[1]

When Faulkner mentioned the topic of a new Lord Lieutenant he was interested, like most Irishmen, in a man who would be a friend to the Irish interest. If Burke had even thought of asking Lord Rockingham to come to Ireland as Lord Lieutenant, he might have had some influence on the state of affairs in Ireland. The Marquess never knowingly applied for the post. At this time King George III expected any candidate for Lord Lieutenant to spend his term of appointment in Ireland. Past governors had come to Ireland every other year to open the Irish Parliament and then had returned to England. Also, the remuneration was small, only £ 3,000 a year. Few men were willing to give up a comfortable life in England for an uncomfortable and possibly an insecure stay in Ireland. The final appointee for the position was Charles Lord Viscount Townshend.[2]

1. 24–27 January 1767.
2. Lecky, *A History of Ireland*, 2:78 ff.

George Faulkner to Edmund Burke
(*Northamptonshire Archives*)

Dublin, January 20, 1767

Dear Sir

The great Pleasure I have in your being presented with the Freedom of this City is the Cause of my troubling you with this Letter to congratulate with you thereon. All your Friends here are extreamly joyful on this Occasion, particularly your Friends Counsellors Howard and Ridge,[3] whom I saw Yesterday, as I did my Lord Mayor at the Mansion House last Night, who gave a most superb and grand Ball, which was the brilliantest I ever saw in Beauties, fine Attire and Jewels, greatly superior to any that I have seen at St. James's, Guildhall, the London Mansion House, the Castle of Dublin, or any other Place. All the rest of the World could not produce the same Number of fine Women and clever Fellows in one Assembly as appeared there, the Company amounting to more than 1200 People, some tell me more than 1300. My Lord Mayor, who is a most polite, well bred Gentleman told me he would write to you on your being presented with your Freedom. Never did any Man obtain this Freedom with more Honour and Unanimity than you have done, which hath given me the highest Pleasure. Dr. Leland,[4] your other Friends and I, never meet together that we do not toast your Health in Bumpers. The worthy O'Connor,

Author of The Dissertations on The Irish History, always talks of you with the greatest Respect, and the high Honour you did him in visiting of him. All Affairs are quiet in Ireland, no White or Oakboys[5] being up, notwithstanding the Dearness of Provisions. I have been told by more than one Judge of Assize that the Case of the Riots in Munster is very truly stated. I suppose you have seen this Pamphlet, if not, if you desire, I will send it to you.[6] By this Post I send you Watson's Almanack, which is the present State of Ireland. All the Chat here at present is, upon the Tryal of the Earl of Ely[7] for Idiocy. His Lordship hath 40,000 £ in ready Cash, and an Estate of more than 11,000 £ a Year, above 3000 £ a year of which is in the Right of his Mother, who was Daughter to Sir Gustavus Hume, Bart,[8] whom Mr. Loftus, late Earl of Ely married, as did Mr. George Rochfort, Brother to the Earl of Belvedere, the other Daughter. The Prosecution is carrying on at the Suit of Mr. Rochfort to endeavour to prove his Lordship (now 28 years old) an Idiot, and to prevent his levying Fines, and suffering Recoveries. There are ten of the most eminent Lawyers, five on each Side, for both Parties; ten Commissioners of great Worth and Honour, and a most respectable Jury of vast Property, such as Messrs. Conolly, Gardiner, Sir Harry Cavendish[9] and others of mighty Estates for Commoners. I attended the Tryal Yesterday for five Hours, which was adjourned to this Day, and is further adjourned, and will take up many Days more, in examining Witnesses. I shall take up no more of your Time on this Account, but refer you to your Friends the Lawyers who have been retained and refreshed in this Cause.

I wish you would prevail on the Marquis and Lady Rockingham to come hither as Lord and Lady Lieutenant. His Lordship's good Sense and Candor, and my Lady's excessive Beauty, Politeness, Freedom and Ease, would captivate the whole Kingdom; and pray do you come with them in the Station of First Secretary for the Honour of the Marquis and the Benefit of this Country.

Dr. Leland, who proposeth to be in London next March, presenteth his Compliments and Respects to you, and I beg you will be pleased to do the same in my Name to Mrs. Burke, which will very much oblige.

Your most obedient and

most humble Servant

George Faulkner

3. Gorges Edmond Howard (1715–1786), lawyer and essayist. John Ridge, Irish lawyer related to Edmund Burke and friend of Goldsmith and the Johnson coterie.

4. Thomas Leland (1722–1785), D.D., Senior Fellow at Trinity College, Dublin; best known for his *History of Ireland from the Invasion of Henry the Second* (1773).

5. Lecky, *A History of Ireland*, 2:34 ff. The Oakboys were Protestant resisters of the Road Act which demanded that highways be repaired by the personal labor of the housekeepers. The Oakboys were restricted to the northern provinces of Armagh and Tyrone. The Whiteboys arose in Munster against tithing and land enclosure.

6. See the review by Anonymous, "A Candid Inquiry into the Causes and Motives of the Late Riots in Munster in Ireland," pp. 32–34.

7. *Dublin Journal*, 24–27 January 1767, gives the following account: "On Monday the 19th Inst. came on at the Lying-in Hospital a most remarkable Trial grounded on a Suggestion made by George Rochfort, Esq., of the Idiocy of Nicholas Hume, Earl of Ely.

"The presiding Commissioners were: The Right Hon. Hercules Langford Rowley, the Right Hon. William Brownalow, Charles Walker and Francis Veley [sic] Esq., two of the Masters of Chancery. George Smyth, Esq., one of his Majesty's Council at Law; Arthur Pomeroy, Esq.; Richard Howard, Esq.; William Sharman, Esq.; and Alderman Percival Hunt. The jury were: The Rt. Hon. Charles Gardiner, Rt. Hon. Thomas Conolly, Hon. William Brabazon, Sir Henry Cavendish, Bart.; Thomas Cobbe, Esq.; Henry Mitchell, Esq.; Charles Leslie, Esq.; John Pullard, Esq.; Phil. Crampton, Esq.; Ben. Geale, Esq.; Ben. Barton, Esq., aldermen of Dublin. The Examination of Witnesses employed five Days; and on Saturday the 24th, the Earl of Ely himself was examined by the Commissioners in the Presence of the said George Rochfort, and of two Council on the part of the Petitioner, and two on the Part of the Earl; and after an Examination of three quarters of an Hour upwards, the Jurors without Debate returned their Verdict, that Nicholas Hume Earl of Ely is *not an Idiot* or of unsound Mind. The Commissioners unanimously approved the Verdict and have returned the Inquisition into the High Court of Chancery."

8. Baronet of Castle Hume, County Fermanagh.

9. The Right Honourable Thomas Conolly (1738–1803), Privy Councillor of Ireland and related by marriage to the Duke and Duchess of Leinster; Sir Harry Cavendish, Teller of the Irish Exchequer.

GEORGE FAULKNER TO SAMUEL DERRICK § The letters between George Faulkner and Samuel Derrick (1724–1769), Irish poet and successor to "Beau" Nash as master of ceremonies at Bath, span a period of eight years. The correspondence lapses after May 1761. Faulkner wrote one more letter to Derrick in 1766 when Derrick was "King of Bath."

George Faulkner to Samuel Derrick
(*Victoria and Albert Museum, London, Forster 146, 40*)

Dublin, July 5, 1757

Dear Sir

I have been favoured with two very kind and polite Letters from you since my Return hither, to which you should have had immediate Answers had I not in some Hurry and Confusion mislaid your first with some others, which I hope will plead my Excuse and procure my Pardon; and the Journal should have been sent but for the above Reason; but for the Future, I believe you will receive it constantly, if not, pray let me know. I thank you for your Intelligence and Politics, and request the Favour of your most agreeable and entertaining Correspondence, and shall be obliged to you for the Continuance of it.

I am very glad of your undertaking the Publication and Writing the Notes to Dryden's Works which you mention, and most heartily wish you Success in that Copy.[1] I thank you very heartily for your kind offer to me of neat Copy Work which I am very sorry I can not accept of, being for some time past in a very indifferent State of Health, which maketh me rather decline than pursue Business and besides Reading is so much out of Fashion in Ireland, that at a Meeting of the most eminent Booksellers here, it was positively declared, that not one Book or Pamphlet that hath been printed or published here for seven years past, excepting in the late Dispute between the Patriot and Court parties have quit cost. And, how should it be otherwise, when most of

49

our young Nobility and Gentry are educated at the Schools and Universities of England, Geneva, and some in Germany, to the great Loss and Injury of this Country, which I believe is now the most miserable in Europe, owing to our Absentees, the Want of Trade, and most Provisions of Life, which have been for a long Time past, much dearer than in any other Part of Europe.

Mr. John Smith, Bookseller in Dame-street published all Dryden's Poems in two Volumes, twelvemo, closely printed, some years ago,[2] which perhaps you have not seen; if not, they may be of some Use to you, and I will send them by the first opportunity, directed to you at the Bedford or the Smyrna Coffee-houses. If you go on with this Work, I think it would not be amiss to write to Smith, as he may think it an Innovation upon his property if any one else should reprint your Edition.

How happy are you in the pleasing, agreeable, polite, entertaining and improving company of Dr. Hart,[3] Mr. Mallet,[4] Dr. Smollett, and the other shining Men of the Age, with whom I very often wish to be; but as Fate has confined me to this Place, I make it most agreeable to me, having the Conversation of Men of Wit, Learning and Taste, although very few of them are Authors, well knowing that Ireland cannot pay Men of their Merit or Labours. All Parties are very quiet here at present, there being nothing to quarrel about, but warm work is expected next Session. When you see Dr. Brooke,[5] pray make my best Wishes and Compliments to him and his agreeable Family and to call at the Bedford and Smyrna and to the above named Gentlemen, which would oblige your most obedient humble Servant.

George Faulkner

Barry and Macklin called this day.[6]

1. Faulkner did not publish an Irish edition of Dryden's *Works*. However, he did advertise for subscriptions for Derrick's project in his *Dublin Journal*, 27 February–3 March 1759, that "Proposals for printing for Subscription, *Miscellanies in Prose and Verse*, consisting of Plays, Poems, Satire, Essays and Translations. By Samuel Derrick. . . . Subscriptions are taken in by Mr. George Faulkner in Essex-street, Dublin; Mr. Dodsley in Pall-Mall; and by the Author at the Smyrna Coffee House, Pall Mall, London."

2. Derrick mentions in his Preface to his edition of *The Miscellaneous Works of John Dryden* (London: J. and R. Tonson, 1760); 1:vii, that Smith, the Irish printer, had been the last man to publish a collection of Dryden's poetry in 1742. It seems reasonable to believe that Faulkner sent Derrick the copy of Smith's edition as he had promised in this letter.

3. Walter Harte (1709–1774), Canon of Windsor, poetical imitator of Alexander Pope, and friend of Dr. Johnson.

4. David Mallet or Malloch (1705–1765), Scottish playwright and minor poet. It is conceivable that Faulkner met Mallet as early as 1745. Faulkner states in his *Dublin Journal*, 9–13 July 1745, that "we are likewise informed that the ingenious Mr. Mallet, who is the author of the Life of Lord Bacon, and several poetical Pieces . . . will come over with the Lord Lieutenant."

5. Henry Brooke (1703–1783), Irish playwright, novelist, and pamphleteer. He is best known for his two plays *Gustavus Vasa* and *Essex* and his novel *Fool of Quality*.

6. Spranger Barry (1719–1777), Irish tragedian and playhouse manager. He and Thomas Woodward were co-managers of the new Crow Street Theater. Charles Macklin (1697–1797), Irish actor and playwright. Woodward replaced Macklin as Barry's co-manager.

George Faulkner to Samuel Derrick
(Forster 146, 41)

Dublin, Nov. 16, 1758

Dear Sir,

You are extreamly kind in thinking of a Friend at this Distance, who is very much obliged to you for your kind Remembrance of him. I most heartily thank you for your theatrical News, which was very agreeable and entertaining; and wish it were in my Power to send you some Account of ours. Barry, Woodward and his Wife were to have dined with me last Sunday at my Villa; the former disappointed me, but the latter were punctual, with eight or ten other agreeable Friends. Mr. and Mrs. Woodward (notwithstanding it is the Month of November) were in Raptures at my Gardens, Improvements and Serpentine River, gliding and meandering, rushing, foaming, roaring and all the Beauties that can be formed by Water. The new Theatre meets with good Success. The old keepeth its Ground to the Astonishment of the World, having no capital Players of either Sex, but expect strong Reinforcements from Abroad by Diggs and Mrs. Ward, Sheridan and Mrs. Fitzhenry,[1] who, I look upon to be the best Actress of her Age. We have got one Brown, who is a most surprizing Comedian, and hath played the Copper Captain in Rule a Wife and Have a Wife, several Times to very crowded Audiences to their entire Satisfaction. But, as you correspond with Mr. Weeks,[2] who is the greatest theatrical critic that I know, I make no Doubt, but he sendeth you the best Accounts. I must beg your Acceptance of a Sett of Swift's Works, and that you will give them a Place in your Study. They shall be sent as you direct by the first Opportunity.

You know that Dublin is the poorest Place in the World for Subscriptions to Books. It is much easier to get an hundred Dinners, with as many dozen Bottles of Claret, than a single Guinea for the best Author, few or no People here caring to subscribe, Reading not being the prevailing Taste at present. However, if you will accept of an Advertisement in my Paper, it is at your Service.[3]

(Sat. 18) Since writing the foregoing, Diggs and Mrs. Ward arrived here Yesterday from Scotland: But we are in much Pain for the Chester Trader, which it is feared is cast away with many Passengers vast Sums of ready Money received at Chester Fair for Linens, large Bales of wrought and raw Silks, Woollens, Hops, Teas, etc. Theophilus Cibber, Maddox, the Rope Dancer and other Tumblers from Sadlers Wells; and also, several fine Scenes and Machines for Pantomines in Sheridan's Theatre, which Losses will be very injurious to him.[4]

Whenever you enter into Business I wish you every Happiness and Success. But can you quit the Muses for sordid Pelf? If you do, I shall not despair of seeing you in Ireland, and at the Linen Hall, buying vast Quantities of Irish Manufactures to be exported to England and other Countries:[5] and whenever you come hither I shall be glad to see you at my Villa which is become the Receptacle for the Literati and all Men of Genius in every Profession, some of whom have written Poems, and others have drawn Plans and Perspective Views of my little Farm with all the adjacent Beauties. I wish Mr. Lambert[6] was to see it, and take a Landscape from it: If he did, his great Genius and masterly Pencil would make it far superior to Mount Edgcumb.[7] Whenever you see that Gentleman, my dear and worthy old Friend Clarke[8] and many others that may remember me at the Smyrna, Bedford or anywhere else, pray make my Compliments to them; and believe me to be with greatest Truth and Esteem;

Your sincere well-wisher, and most obedient humble Servant,

George Faulkner

Your Correspondence being so very agreeable I shall be glad to hear from you, and hope the Letters may be very long, London affording more Variety for different Subjects, and Dublin less than any great City in Europe.

If you will be at the Trouble of calling on Messieurs Davys and Reymer[9] in Holborn with my Compliments to them both, pray desire them to give you one of Dr. Lawson's Lectures,[10] which hath sold better and is more liked by all People than any Book I have published since Swift's Works, and hope they will have an equal Sale.

1. Robert Hitchcock, *Historical View of the Irish Stage*, 1:305. West Digges (1720–1786), gentleman actor, first appeared at Smock Alley in 1749; Sarah Ward had played opposite Digges at Covent Garden; Mrs. Fitzhenry, another London actress, was called "the first actress of her age" by Robert Hitchcock; see Esther Sheldon, *Thomas Sheridan of Smock Valley* (Princeton, N.J.: Princeton University Press, 1967), pp. 229, 248, for the maneuvers by Sheridan to fight off the rival Crow Street Theater.

2. James Eyre Weeks, classmate of Sheridan at Trinity College. He wrote a poem entitled "Rhapsody of the Stage."

3. Faulkner's offer to advertise for Derrick's edition of a Dryden miscellany.

4. Theophilus Cibber drowned in the Irish Sea about 27 October 1758.

5. Faulkner refers to Derrick's early training as a linen draper. He appears to think Derrick will return to being a merchant rather than starve as a hack writer.

6. George Lambert, the British landscape and scenery painter.

7. The county seat in Cornwall of the Earl of Mt. Edgecumbe.

8. The identification is not a positive one. However, the Reverend Henry Clarke was a friend of Swift, and a onetime vice-provost of

Trinity College, Dublin. See Harold Williams's note in Swift, *Corre-spondence*, 4:273.

9. Lockyer Davis and Charles Reymer. See Plomer, *Dictionary of Printers and Booksellers at Work in England, Scotland and Ireland, 1726–1775*, p. 72.

10. John Lawson (1712–1759), D.D., writer and lecturer in Oratory at Trinity College, Dublin. Faulkner advertised Lawson's *Lectures Concerning Oratory* "speedily will be published" in the *Dublin Journal*, 14–17 October 1758. One assumes that Faulkner, with his customary delay, had the books for sale by the first of the following month. It is uncertain as to whether Faulkner printed this book or whether Reymer and Bowyer in London shipped it to Dublin where Faulkner printed a frontispiece and bound the book for his customers.

George Faulkner to Samuel Derrick
(Forster 146, 42)

Dublin, April 5, 1759

Dear Sir

Your last polite, agreeable and entertaining Letter, gave me and many others to whom I shewed it, more Pleasure than I can express; and, all think that, I am so very happy in your Correspondence, that I am their Envy. Your Epistles are modern History, wrote in the most elegant Style, and your Anecdotes more pleasing than Words can express. Messieurs Barry, Woodward and Mrs. Woodward dined with me the Sunday after I had received your Letter, which I shewed them; for which they are much obliged to you for your kind Remembrance of them, and desire their Compliments to you in Return. Barry hath been very Ill of a Fever for some Time past, and hath almost gone through the whole Decade of Physic by severe Blisters, Bleedings, Vomittings, Clysters, etc., and is not yet recovered: However, they have had great Success at the new Theatre, by Woodward's indefatigable Industry in playing not only in every Comedy, but in every Farce, as well as the Harlequin in the Entertainment of Fortunatus, which hath had a prodigious great Run, the Scenes and Machinery being very fine. They have great Benefits at the Theatre Royal, as well as in Crow-Street, as we could, if Garrick were here, make up the best Company of Players in the World.

We hear much of Sheridan's Success at London, Oxford and Cambridge which I hope is True, as I wish him every Happiness.

The Tallow and live Cattle Bills are much disliked by all the People of this Kingdom, as being most injurious to this Nation.

I have advertised your Proposals, which I suppose you have seen in the Journal, and could wish, they had answered your Expectations and mine, according to my sincere Desires; but, as I formerly told you, Dublin is no Place for Subscriptions: However, the Honourable Robert Marshall, Esq., one of the Judges of the Common Pleas hath subscribed and paid me half a Guinea and please to put down my Name for Six. I suppose you hear often from Wilks,[1] who can give you a much better Account of theatrical Affairs than I can possibly do, as he is very active, and I and [sic] Invalid and a Criple. Did you get Lawson's Lectures from Mr. Davys? And how do you like them? Dr. Delany says, they are finest Performance in this or the last Century. Dunkin[2] carryeth his Praises much higher, by saying there hath not been so good a Work for five Centuries past, upon which and Lawson's Death he is writing a Poem, which I wish I could send you by Post: Lawson ordered by his Will that all his Writings should be burned, which was accordingly done by his Executors.

Our Town is very empty and dull at present, all the Judges and many Lawyers being on Circuit.

I had almost forgot to tell you that Lord Chesterfield and Waldegrave[3] are in the highest Raptures with Lawson's Lectures. Pray let me know what they say of them in London, which will very much oblige your very affectionate and most obedient humble Servant

George Faulkner

My best Wishes and Compliments to Messieurs Harte, Clarke, Lockman[4] and my other Friends that may inquire for me.

1. Thomas Wilkes wrote a *General View of the Stage* (London: Printed for J. Coote, in Paternoster Row and W. Whetstone in Skinner Row, Dublin, 1759). Esther Sheldon mistakenly assigns this book to Samuel Derrick. It is possible that he may have written part of it; see W. J. Lawrence, *Times Literary Supplement* (June 26, 1930). Wilkes also was the Dublin editor for Faulkner's Dublin edition of Swift's letters in *Works*, volumes 14–16 (1767) octavo.

2. William Dunkin (1709–1765), D.D., poet and friend of Faulkner and Lord Chesterfield. Chesterfield had Dunkin appointed as headmaster of Portora Royal School, Enniskillen.

3. James Waldegrave, second Earl Waldegrave (1715–1763); future tutor of George III; confidant of George II, 1743–1760.

4. John Lockman (1698–1771), miscellaneous writer and translator. He was a friend and colleague of Dr. Thomas Birch, secretary of the Royal Society. Lockman helped Birch with the *General Dictionary* (1734–1741).

George Faulkner to Samuel Derrick
(Forster 146, 43)

Dublin, Dec. 18, 1759

Dear Sir

Both your pleasing Letters of the 1st and 7th Instant, and that for Mr. Wilks came by yesterday's Mail. That Gentleman hath got much Reputation by his Writing on the Stage. I am very glad that Swift's Works are safe in London, as Books printed here are liable to Seizure in England. I sent a Letter with them wherein I desired you when you got to Bath to send me a List of such People from Ireland as were there, and if I knew any of them, I would write to them in your Favour.¹ I also told you, that I did not know the Author of the Verses, that you enquired after, being sent to me by Post from the Country.

The Suspension of your most agreeable and entertaining Correspondence was a very great Loss to me, and I shall endeavor to keep it up as much as beth in my Power. Indeed the People of Ireland who are most remarkable for their Credulity, were Infidels with Regard to the French Invasion being intended for this Kingdom, which they might ravage, burn and plunder, but could never keep whilst England had a Superiority at Sea; and there is such Spirit of Loyalty and Bravery in this Nation, that few or none of the French could escape; The Roman Catholics of all the great cities here, addressing and entering into Associations in Support of his Majesty, his crown and his Dignity. The trifling Riots that happened here did not proceed from Disloyalty, but from a Rumor, that there was to be an Union between Great Britain and Ireland; That no more Parliaments were to be held here; That our Nobility and Gentry would live in England; That Dublin would be depopulated, and that Grass would grow in the Streets; which Reports alarmed the Common or Lower People so much, that they assembled in great numbers on College Green, and stopped the Lord Chancellor,[2] the Bishop of Killalla[3] in their Coaches, and Lord Inchiquin[4] in his chair: the Attorney General[5] in his Chariot, and three or four other Members of the House of Commons, asking them to swear, and offering a Book to them (which was the first Volume of the Spectator, which your Friend Mr. Woodward[6] was reading at the Window opposite to the Parliament House, which the Rabble took for a Bible) to swear that they would never propose, or consent to an Union with Great Britain; but the Lord Mayor and Sheriffs appearing soon after and a Troop of Horse being sent by the Duke of Bedford,[7] they all went Home very quietly, without doing the least Damage excepting as before mentioned.[8]

I sincerely wish you Success in your History of Ireland which I shall be very glad to see from your Pen, as you write a good Style, and will be impartial. I should be very glad it were in my Power to give you any aid or assistance, but, all I can do, is to recommend to you to read the undernamed Authors and Compilers,[9] to wit, Hollingshed's Chronicle. Sir James Ware's Works. O'Conor's and Keating's Histories of Ireland. Carte's Life of the Duke of Ormond. Aristotle, who made honourable Mention of Ireland in the Time of Alexander. Venerable Bede. Sir John Davis's Account of Ireland. Lord Castlehaven's Memoirs. The Parliamentary Journals of England and Ireland. Harris's History of the Counties of Down, and his other collections in three Volumes, Folio. Stanihurst's de Rebus in Hibernia, etc. Heron. Cox's History.

Cambden's [*sic*] Brittannia. Nicholson's Historical Library. Rimer's Foedera particularly the three last Volumes, and examine the Index to that Work. Giraldus Cambrensis. Cambrensus Eversus. Smith's Histories of the Counties of Cork, Kerry and Waterford. Lodge's Peerage of Ireland. Orrery's State Letters, all the Acts of Attainder in England and Ireland which [would] be most useful to you. Phenix Britannicus. Morrison's History. Hibernia Pecata. Hammer's Chronicle. Clanrickard's Life and Letters. Clarendon's ditto. Molyneux's State of Ireland. Swift's Papers relating to ditto. Howell's Letters. O'Conor's Dissertations, and many others that I cannot at present recollect. I am told there is a very good History of Ireland lately published in France, 2 Volumes, quarto, wrote by an Irish Jesuit[10] which is in very great Reputation. I have lately heard that Mr. Brooke hath been offered two thousand guineas to write an History and that he is now upon that work.[11] There are two Gentlemen here, most learned in the Irish Language, Dr. Fergus,[12] an eminent Physician and Dr. Sullivan,[13] a Fellow of our University, and an eminent Advocate.

Our Theatre in Crow-Street meeteth with wonderful Success; and no Wonder, when they have, excepting Garrick, the best Players in the World, Barry, (Messrs.) Woodword and Foot,[14] Mrs. Fitzhenry and Dancer.[15] They received in the Week of the Riot (which hindered many people from going to the plays) above 62.

Last Week I sent you, under Mr. Cowper's Cover, Dunkin's Funeral Obsequies on Lawson's Death;[16] the Dedication to which is much admired for its Wit and Humour, and the Poetry for Smoothness and fine Imagination; but, I think from extream, partiality, few or no Writings of Ireland, please in England, but whatever is wrote in Scotland, is Superior to all others in the World; for so we are told in all Magazines and Reviews. I sold the first Edition of Lawson's Lectures in a very few months, have almost disposed of the second, and am preparing for a third. If you should come to Dublin, I shall be extreamly glad to see you. I just now recollect, that the first Duke of Chandos had the best Collection of Irish Books, Histories and Manuscripts ever known, which with his fine Library were sold to Osborne of Gray's Inn.[17] Enquire of him to whom he disposed of them. I have not room to mention Friends particularly, but pray make my best Wishes and Compliments to them all, which will oblige your most obedient and humble Servant,

George Faulkner

1. Derrick became master of ceremonies in Bath in 1762. It would appear that he was already asking friends to write letters to important people in Bath that he might succeed Beau Nash as master of ceremonies.

2. John Bowes (1690–1767), Lord Chancellor of Ireland (1757), became Baron Clonlyon (1758) and Lord Chief Justice (1765).

3. Richard Robinson (1709–1794), D.D., Bishop of Kilala (1752–1759) and Primate of Ireland (1765), and Baron Rokeby of Armagh (1777).

4. William O'Brien, sixth Earl of Inchiquin.

5. No positive identification, possibly Anthony Malone.

6. Thomas Woodward, co-manager of the Crow Street Theater.

7. John Russell, fourth Duke of Bedford (1710–1771).

8. Compare with Tobias Smollett, *The History of England from the Revolution until the Death of George the Second*, 4:509.

9. The following list shows the wide acquaintanceship George Faulkner had with the pertinent histories of his time: Raphael Holinshed, *The Chronicles of England, Scotland and Ireland* (London, 1577) [Faulkner, no doubt, had seen the London 1728 edition by Dr. Drake]; James Ware, *De Hibernia Antiquitatibus, ejus Disquisitiones* (London, 1654); idem in English, *Antiquities and the History of Ireland*, trans. Walter Harris (Dublin, 1705); Dermod O'Conor, *The General History of Ireland* (Dublin and London, 1723); Thomas Carte, *A History of the Life of James, Duke of Ormonde* (London, 1736–1735 [sic]); Aristotle *De Mundo* 293b, 13; Sir John Davies, *A Discoverie of the True Cause Why Ireland Was Never Entirely Subdued until His Majestie's Raigne* (London, 1612; Dublin, 1613, 1644); James Touchet, Earl of Castlehaven, and Lord Audley, *Memoirs* (London, 1680); *The Parliamentary History of England to 1660*, 24 vols. (London, 1751–1752); Walter Harris and Charles Smith, *The Ancient and Present State of the City and the County of Down* (Dublin, 1744); Charles Smith, *Ancient and Present State of the County and City of Waterford* (Dublin, 1746); Charles Smith, *Ancient and Present State of Kerry* (Dublin, 1756); John Lodge, *Peerage of Ireland or a Genealogical History of the Present Nobility*, 4 vols. (London, 1754); Roger Boyle, First Earl of Orrery, *A Collection of the State Papers of Roger Boyle* . . . (Dublin, 1742); *Phenix Britannicus*, ed. S. Morgan (London, 1732); Fynes Morrison, *An Itinerary Written by Fynes Morrison Containing His Ten Yeeres Travell Through the Twelve Dominions of Germany, Bohemia* . . . *France, England, Scotland, and Ireland*, in three parts (London, 1617) [Second Part with Chapter Five of Third part reprinted as *History of Ireland*, 2 vols. (Dublin, 1735)]; Sir Thomas Straf-

ford, *Paccata Hibernia, or The Late Warres of Ireland especially in Munster under The Government of Sir George Carew* (London, 1633); Meredith Hammer, *Chronicle of Ireland* (Dublin, 1633), folio, republished in Sir James Ware's *History of Ireland*; Richard Stanihurst, *De Rebus in Hibernia Gestes, Libri Quattuor* (Antwerp, 1584); Thomas Cox, *Magna Britannia et Hibernia et Nova, or a New Survey of Great Britain,* collected and compared by an impartial hand (English Counties), 6 vols. (London, 1720–1731); Bede, *Historia Ecclesiatica Anglorum,* ed. A. Whelock (Cantabrigiae, 1643); William Camden, *Britannia: sive florentissimorum regnorum Angliae, Scotiae, Hiberniae Chorographia descriptio,* two parts (Frankfurt, 1590); William Nicholson, *The Irish Historical Library* (London, 1724); Thomas Rymer, *Foedera Conventiones, Literae et cujus eunque geheris, acta publica inter regis Angliae, et alias, quos vis imperatores Riges Pontifices Principes vel Comunitatis,* ed. G. Homes, 20 vols. (London, 1727–1735); Giraldus Cambrensis, *Topographia Hiberniae: sive de Mirabilibus Hiberniae* (London, 1602), included in Camden's *Britannia;* John Lynch, *Cambrensis Eversus: seu potius historica fides in rebus Hiberbicus Giraldus Cambrensis Abrigada* (Dublin, 1662); Clanrickard, *Life and Letters of Ulrick, Marquis of Clanrickard . . . Lord Lieutenant of Ireland and Commander in Chief of King Charles during the Rebellion* (London, 1757); Edward Hyde, Earl of Clarendon, *The History of the Rebellion and Civil Wars in England* (Oxford, 1702–1704); William Molyneux, *The Case of Ireland's being Bound by An Act of Parliament in England, Stated* (Dublin, 1697); James Howell, *Mercurius Hibernius: Or a Discourse of the Late Insurrection in Ireland* (Bristol, 1644).

10. Abbe MacGeoghegan, *Histoire de L'Irlande, Ancienne et Moderne, tirée des monuments le plus authentique* (Paris, 1758). See supra, Faulkner's letter to O'Conor, 8 August 1763.

11. Faulkner was misinformed. Brooke did not write a history of Ireland. See Gilbert, "Correspondence and Mss of Charles O'Conor," *Appendix to the Eighth Report,* 7:442. O'Conor had entrusted Brooke with some Irish manuscripts called *Oygygian Tales;* Brooke, in 1744, advertised these manuscripts as a new *History of Ireland,* which he never realized.

12. John Fergus, M.D., the best known Catholic physician in Dublin. He sold his collection of Irish books and manuscripts to Trinity College, Dublin.

13. Francis Stoughton Sullivan (1719–1776), Irish jurist and a Senior Fellow at Trinity College, Dublin.

14. Samuel Foote.

15. Ann Dancer, an actress at Crow Street Theater.

16. See supra, Faulkner to Derrick, 16 November 1758. Lawson died before May 1759. Faulkner first advertised a pamphlet on 15 May 1759 as *Lawson's Obsequies and Eclogue to which will be Prefixed an Address to the Earl of Chesterfield.* True to his practice of advertising and then waiting, George Faulkner did advertise for sale on 1 January 1760 the same pamphlet but with a new title, *An Epistle to the Right Honourable Philip Lord Chesterfield, to which is added Lawson's Obsequies.*

17. Swift, *Correspondence,* 4:250. Professor Williams identified

this as the Sir James Ware manuscripts which Swift hoped to obtain for Trinity College, Dublin. In spite of this, the Duke offered the manuscripts for sale. The materials are now in the British Museum, except for the Rawlinson Mss in the Bodleian.

George Faulkner to Samuel Derrick
(Forster 146, 44)

Dublin, May 8, 1760

Dear Sir

I am extreamly glad to hear of your Introduction to the D. of Newcastle,[1] and the Friendship and Countenance that you meet with from the great Men you mention; and make not the least Doubt, since you have made this happy Acquaintance, which your Merit and Writings have justly entitled you to, that you will make the proper Use of this fine Prospect, by which, I think, it is probable that your Fortune is made, or that you are in a fair way to do it. Catch time by the Forelock!

It is very unkind in you or Mr. Mallet to imagine, that I could ever neglect to serve a Friend, and especially a Gentleman of Mr. Mallet's Genius and Abilities, for whom I have the highest Honour. No I went to the Commissioners more than once, and thought that by their Civilities to me on all Occasions, that I could get the Gingham, but they could not serve me, as the Land Officer had made a Seizure of it: But however, they bade me apply to him, which I did and he agreed to admit it to an Entry, upon having Certificates being sent from the Custom House in London of the Duty being paid there. This the Commissioners told me was all the Indulgence they could possibly grant me; on which I wrote to Mr. Mallet, who, instead of sending attested Certificates from your Custom House, inclosed me some Papers from the Person the Gingham was bought from, which could not be of the least Service, not being the proper Certificates for the Purpose. After this Mr. Mallet wrote to Mr. Mayne,[2] as well as to me, and that Gentleman called on me, when I told him

61

what Steps I had taken, which he approved of, and undertook the Management of that Affair upon himself; that I need not stir anymore on this Occasion; that he would write to the worthy Mr. Mallet by that Post, and set Engines at Work to have the Gingham restored, and carry it with him to England. Since that Time I have not seen Mr. Mayne, who, I flattered myself, would have called on me, as he promised, but I have not seen him since. Thus far I have given an Account of my Commission and shall be very proud to hear from, and, if in my Power, to serve Mr. Mallet on any Occasion. That Gentleman's most excellent Performances deserve the finest Editions in Paper, Print, and Plates, and I have his fine Edition of Edwin and Emma coming to me; and I wrote for some of your Dryden.

Dr. Dunkin, who is an Admirer of your Letters, is now drinking some of the best Claret in the World with me, and we are toasting your Health and Friends. London is a fertile Soil for writing Letters, and Dublin most barren, few Occurrences happening here worth staining Paper with, excepting now and then a few Debates in Parliament, and always having some of the best Players in the World, who have this Winter, met with more Success than can be imagined, both Houses being often filled with most crowded Audiences on the same Night, and even Smock-Alley having sometimes more than that Theatre can contain. The large Sums received at Crow-Street are almost incredible, notwithstanding the Failure of our Banks and Public Credit; but this can be no Wonder, when we have the best Stage in the World, with Barry, Messrs. Woodward, Mrs. Fitzhenry, Dancer, etc. which makes me wonder that London is not quite empty, and all the People of Taste and Affectation not crowding to see Plays acted in Dublin.

Our Parliament are now upon the Regulation of Coin, and endeavouring to give a Currency to the Spanish and Portuguese Coins of Gold and Silver, which perhaps may in some shape cause a Circulation of Cash amongst us, which never was more wanted.

I shall soon send Captain Cruikshank's Account[3] to our Friend Talbot,[4] and hope he is well.

I long much to see my Friends in London, but I cannot drink vile Port, or worse Malt Liquors, but must have the best Claret, and keep a Coach and good Lodgings into the Bargain, but, it is not impossible, that if Money be restored to us, but I may have the Pleasure of seeing you and some other Friends before next Winter, to whom be pleased to make my best Wishes and Compliments from your most affectionate obedient and humble Servant,

George Faulkner

1. Thomas Pelham Holles (1693-1768).
2. Perry Mayne (1700-1761), British admiral and later revenue officer in Ireland.
3. "Captain Cruikshank's account" could very well be the pamphlet entitled *The Conduct and Treatment of John Crookshanks, Esq.*, late commander of His Majesty's ship *Lark*. This pamphlet touched off a minor pamphlet war between Crookshanks and his former commander, Admiral Charles Knowles. Knowles replied to the Crookshank pamphlet in one entitled *A Refutation of the Charge brought against Admiral Knowles in a Late Pamphlet intitled 'The Conduct and Treatment of John Crookshanks, Esq.'* A reviewer, possibly Tobias Smollet in the *Critical Review* 7 (May 1759): 554 ff., states, "Mr. Knowles in the piece before us, denies every particular of the charge, article by article, ekes out the pamphlet with copies of orders and letters from the Admiralty; and concludes with a letter to him from Mr. Crookshanks, in which that gentleman mentions the *'delicacy*, the *humane* and *genteel behavior that he* (the Admiral) *had shewn him still reserving to himself the dignity and duty of an officer.'* If Mr. Knowles were acquainted with the figure which the Greeks call *Eipuvia*, perhaps he would not interpret this compliment *sur la pied de la lettre*. This mode or trope is like the practice of the waterman who looks one way while he rows the other."
4. There is no positive identification of this man.

George Faulkner to Samuel Derrick

(Forster 146, 45)

Dublin, Sept. 18, 1760

Dear Sir

I most heartily congratulate with you on your safe Arrival in your native Country, which I hope may be agreeable to you and your entertaining traveling Friend, and am very sorry your Arrival was not sooner, as it would have given me an Opportunity of indulging myself in your most agreeable Company.

Your Complaints of our Inns are too just, which I experienced this Time 12 Month, in a Journey to and from Kinssale, the Sight of which fine Harbour and the many delightful Seats and fine Situations made Amends for the Want of Elegance and Cleanliness.[1] There is an English Gentleman, now at my Elbow, who swears that naked Legs and Feet, are more agreeable, sweet and cleanly than stinking Toes and dirty Legs bound up and sweathed in tight Shoes and dirty stocking Feet, which send forth unsavoury Smells to the no small Annoyance of Noses. The poor People who have no artificial Covering for their Limbs wash them every Day, and particularly before they go to Bed; whereas those who have them bound up in these Bandages very seldom use Water to supple their Joints. However, I am no Advocate for Sluttishness, and wish, it were the Custom of this poor Country to have as neat People and as good Inns, as in the rich and flourishing Kingdom of England. But had you gone to the adjoining northern Kingdom you would have had more Cause of Complaints against that Country than this, by all that I have heard and read. But pray tell me sincerely is not the Lake of Killarney superior to all Beauties of Nature, that you ever saw before? And can there be Beauty without Contrast? Or Painting without Light and Shade? I have no Part of Life to upbraid myself with, but my Neglect of seeing this wonderful Killarney, and the Giant's Causeway, both which exceed all other Curiosities in Nature. I advertised twice for a Party to go to the latter Place, but I did not succeed, however, if please God, I live until next Summer I will go, with only my own Servant. Do not fail to write a Definition of this Lake, which will be a finer Subject for a Poem than Windsor Forest, Cowper's Hill, Stowe, or any Place in England. The Situation of Kilkenny is fine. The Castle on a fine Height with beautiful Prospects of Woods, Lawns, Hills, Dales, Water, and every other View to enrich a Landscape. The old Buildings at Leighlin Bridge,[2] the Castle at Carlow, the Ruins at Castle Dermot,[3] the Vestiges of the famous Earl of Strafford's House at Gigginstown or Jillianstown,[4] and the Danish Mount at Naas, with other Views as you approach Dublin, will not be disagreeable, where, I shall hope for the Pleasure of seeing you and Mr. Willoughby,[5] very soon, as I am obliged to go to England very soon,[6] and therefore most earnestly request, that you will favour me with your Company as much as you can during my Stay. You must see Powers Court, the Waterfall and the Dargall before you leave us, near which I can promise you will meet with good Food and Wine.

I am now going abroad to Dinner where according to Custom and Irish Hospitality, I most joyfully spend the Evening, and could wish that you and Mr. Willoughby were of the Party, and am Dear Sir, your most affectionate obedient and humble Servant.

George Faulkner

Your Box came to hand.

1. Faulkner suggested to Derrick an itinerary for Derrick's trip from Killarney to Dublin. Faulkner never mentioned going as far west as Killarney and thus limited his comments to places that he had seen on his own trip from Kinsale, on the south coast, to Dublin. Faulkner would have Derrick travel through what are the modern towns of Kilkenny, Carlow, and Naas. Derrick's return to Ireland at this time became a major source for his book *Letters Written from Leverpool, Chester, Corke, the Lake of Killarney, Dublin, Tunbridge-Wells and Bath* (1767). Faulkner advertised this book for sale in his *Dublin Journal*, 14–18 July 1767.
2. South of Carlow.
3. North of Carlow.
4. Halfway between Carlow and Naas.
5. No positive identification.
6. See supra, Faulkner to Derrick, 4 October 1760. Faulkner left Dublin on 5 October, before Derrick arrived.

George Faulkner to Samuel Derrick
(Forster 146, 44)

Dublin, Oct. 4, 1760

Dear Sir

Your most agreeable travelling Letter is come to Hand, and is very entertaining; but, I should have been much better pleased had you been here before this Time, as I should have had an opportunity of waiting on you to the Waterfall and the Dargel, which I am very confident would have been very agreeable to you and Mr. Willoughby. I had the Happiness of spending Thursday and Friday at my Lord Powerscourt's fine Seat with your Friend Lord Charlemont, and some Ladies and Gentlemen, where we were entertained in the most polite, hospitable, easy, and agreeable Manner, which Words cannot express, nor the many luxuriant Beauties of Art, as well as Nature, which surround his Lordship's House. I mention Art because there is not a Palace in Europe can produce an Edifice equal to his Egyptian Salon. I shall say no more of these Beauties but leave them to your poetical Imagination to paint them in their proper Colours.

When you go to see these unparalleled Scenes of Delight, in order to make a Contrast, go through Mastown and Kilgobbin, to the House, then to the Waterfalls, from thence to the Dargel, afterwards through the Commons of Bray to Loughnanstown, where there is a little neat House with good Entertainment; and if mine Host at the Inn, Owen Bray be in good Spirits, he will entertain you with an agreeable Song and good Fruit. After this you will have but a short Journey to Dublin.

I am excessively concerned that I can not have the Pleasure of seeing you and Mr. Willoughby before I set for England, which will be to-morrow, but shall hope for that Favour at my Return, which I hope, will be in a Month. In the meantime, I hope, that you will be pleased to call at my house in Essex Street, from whence I shall soon be turned out by the Parliament to make a fine Street from Essex Bridge to Cork Hill.

66

This Day I had a Letter from our Friend Harry Clarke, the enclosed Part of which is relative to you. I am, wishing you every Pleasure and Happiness,

> Your very affectionate most
> humble Servant
> George Faulkner

I answered your former Letter which I suppose may be in the Post Office at Kilkenny.

George Faulkner to Samuel Derrick
(Forster 146, 47)

London, Dec. 2, 1760

Dear Sir

I am extreamly sorry you were so dilatory in going to Dublin as it deprived me of the Happiness of seeing you, and of shewing you the Civilities of the Place. It hath given me very great Concern to hear of your Illness, of which I shall be glad you are quite recovered, and restored to your former Health.

I should have answered your kind Epistle sooner, but waited to give you the best account I could of your Friends, of which you have many here. Lord Corke[1] hath been very ill ever since I came thither, but is now on the mending Hand: His Lordship is much yours and speaketh most affectionately and friendly of you and so doth your worthy Friend, Lord Southwell[2] who talketh of you in Raptures and Panegyricks, but cannot agree with you in your Criticisms on Powerscourt House; the Faults you have found he hath made Beauties of, and will convince you thereof, whenever he has the pleasure of seeing you. Your Friend, Dr. Hart is very ill at Bath, and not expected in London this Winter. Mr. Mallet is not yet come to Town. Your Friends at the Bedford and Smyrna are all very well and greet you with a loving Kiss. I am still

67

in the Circle of old Friends, with an Addition of many new, who are Men of Literature, Wit, and Genius.

Sheridan carries all before him, the House being quite filled by Four, whenever he plays. The Minor hath a mighty Run, by which, and Sheridan, Garrick will make an Immensity, as all People run to see these two famous Actors play together.[3]

Jones[4] hath altered Essex, which is to be acted at Covent Garden.

I am very glad you were so well entertained at Kilkenny by the sawing Mill. Mr. Ockenden[5] hath all the Merit you mention, and you would find more if you knew him better.

The Press hath received a fatal Wound through the Sides of Dr. Smollet, who, I am told, hath received Sentence from Lord Mansfield to be imprisoned three Months, fined 100 £ and to give Security for his Behaviour for seven Years to come, for what he wrote against Admiral Knowles.[6] As to Politics I leave you to the public papers. I am extreamly glad of the good agreement between you and your Aunt, and wish a continuance of it. I suppose you are free of the Dublin Theatres, and well entertained at them. Pray make my compliments to Mr. Wilks, who is a Gentleman I should be glad to be much better acquainted with and wish you would help me thereto, and believe me to be with very great esteem, your most obedient and humble Servant,

George Faulkner

1. John Boyle, Earl of Orrery, became Earl of Cork and Orrery on the death of his cousin, Richard Boyle, Earl of Burlington and Cork in 1753.

2. Thomas Southwell, Lord Southwell of Castle-Matress in the Irish peerage; London Stage: 1660–1800, 2, prt. 4: 353, 765, 807, 821, 825, 834.

3. Judging from several of Faulkner's statements to Derrick, much of his information is hearsay. For example, Faulkner's statement concerning Sheridan, Garrick, and the play The Minor is confusing. The Minor opened at Foote's Little Haymarket Theater on 28 June 1760. When the Haymarket closed for the year, Garrick produced it at Drury Lane. There is no record of either Garrick or Thomas Sheridan playing in it; Sheldon, Sheridan of Smock Alley, pp. 258–63, states that Sheridan worked on "shares" with Garrick, i.e., Sheridan paid the expenses of the theater for the night that he acted and then di-

vided the profits with Garrick for a previously agreed-upon percentage. Garrick and Sheridan did act together in *The Fair Penitent* on 20 November. No doubt Faulkner confused the two plays.

4. "The Bricklayer Poet" is Henry Jones (1721-1770), best known for his play *Essex* which opened at Covent Garden on 23 February 1753. Henry Brooke also wrote a play called *Essex* to which Garrick wrote the epilogue. Garrick played this at Drury Lane on 31 December 1760 and from 3 January to 24 February 1761. Again Faulkner must have confused the two plays.

5. Unidentified.

6. See Lewis Mansfield Knapp, *Tobias Smollett*, pp. 214, 230; see also Alice Parker, "Tobias Smollett and the Law," *Studies in Philology* 39 (1942): 550-53.

George Faulkner to Samuel Derrick
(Forster 146, 48)

London, Jan. 22, 1761

Dear Sir

Weak as mine Eyes are, I will not delay any longer the Satisfaction of writing to you. I have seen your noble Friends, Lords Corke and Southwell several times, and also Mr. Mallet, Mr. Murphy and many others who frequently enquire for you, and speak of you with that Friendship, and Respect that you deserve from all your Friends, by your Merit, Writings and Behaviour. The above Noblemen are much pleased at your Letters, Part of which they have read to me, and say, your Correspondence at this critical Time in Ireland is very pleasing to them. Mr. Mallet is much your Friend, and greatly pleased at your Behaviour and your kind Remembrance. Every Day createth me new Acquaintance, but I never forget the Old. And, I cannot help saying with Pope that "Envy must own I live among the Great."[1] And I will add to it, the Learned, the Gay, the Polite, the Philosopher, the Buck, the Player, the Musician, the Genius, the Artist, the Men of Business, Pleasure etc. but all this and more I must keep in Reserve to have the Happiness of telling you at my Return to Dublin where I hope to have the Pleasure of Saluting you in Essex Street only next Month. In the meantime, I remain your most affectionate and humble Servant.

George Faulkner

1. *Imitations of Horace, Satires* 2:1, 133.

George Faulkner to Samuel Derrick
(Forster 146, 49)

London, Feb. 14, 1761

Dear Sir

I deferred answering your most agreeable and kind Favours of the 27th and 31. past until I could give you some Account of your Friends, who, I can assure you are very numerous and fond of you. I sometimes have the Favour of dining with Lord Southwell at his own House and at Earl Verny's.[1] No Place can be barren of Subjects where ever you are, for your poetical Descriptions are so lively, that they give the highest Pleasure to all those you favour with your Correspondence, particularly to Lord Corke with whom I have the Honour to be very often at his own House and Abroad, as also with the other Noblemen. As to the Disputes between the Privy Councils of England and Ireland I have heard much on both Sides from the Nobles and Commons of each Kingdom. Some People of each Country approve the Spirit of the Irish Council; and others think it is wrong at this Time, there being a War with France, which requires the greatest Unanimity and Force to carry it on at this Time.[2] Upon the whole I think and wish that the People of Ireland, may and ought to have as much Liberty as those of England. I thank you for the Papers between Lord Clonnard and Bisby, with which I not only made many happy hours among my Friends but at the Court of St. James at the King's Levee where I was encircled with blue, green and red Ribbands, Lawn Sleaves, fur and ermine Robes, white Rods, gold Chains, etc. Your definitive Account of the Battle between Captain Connor and Mr. Brenan was very picturesque and humorous. I am very sorry for the murder of the poor innocent Carpenter,[3] and doubt not but Justice will take place. I am very much obliged to you for the account of our Theatres. You say, most truly, that Mr. Wilson[4] is a most worthy and learned Friend, and I will add moreover that he hath a most refined Taste and very great Judgment. Pray make my Compliments to that Gentleman, whom I hope to have the Pleasure of seeing in a very little Time. I shall procure all the Books you desire. You wish to be in London and I long much to be in Dublin, not withstanding the many Entertainments, Connections, and Acquaintance that I have here, many of whom you know, with whom I frequently mingle abroad, sometimes at Taverns, their own House and my Lodgings, which command the most beautiful Prospect of Somerset House, Gardens, the Thames, Westminster Bridge, the Abbey, Parliament House, Whitehall, the delightful rising Ground and Hills of Surry, with the great Variety and Beauties of Yatchts, Lighters, Barges, Boats, etc. crossing to and fro and across the River.[5] You sigh to be with your Friends at the Bedford and Smyrna.

It is here they are humorous, witty, learned and entertaining, and, why should they not? Are they not in the most Universal School of the Globe, where Liberty, Learning, Art, and Sciences go Hand in Hand together? I love them as much as you do, but my own Country much better. No one ever enjoyed more Friendships and Pleasure than I do here among all Degrees of People as you may judge by the following. I have dined on Turtle with Justice Fielding, Foot, Murphy and other most delightful companions. I have supped at your Friend Garrick's, with his most agreeable and amiable Wife at the Head of the Table, which was covered with thirteen Dishes of the most elegant Viands, after which although so very late in the Season, was the finest Dessert of Fruit, mingled with large Pineapples, delicious Grapes, etc. But what were these to the Bill of Company which consisted of Johnson, Coleman, Champion, Loyd, Wilson,[6] Sheridan, Somners[7] and other enchanting Company. Sometimes I spend

71

an agreeable Evening with your worthy Friends Clark, Mallet, Dr. Douglass etc.[8] At other Times I have publick as well as private Invitations; go to Plays, Operas, Burletta's etc. Mr. Mallet hath great Esteem for you. We, according to Custom, eat Fish for Supper, and quaff the best Claret. I am always very glad to hear of the Health and Welfare of my worthy Friend and generous Benefactor Judge Marshall, to whom be pleased to present my best Compliments. Your Friend Jones hath the Muses of his Side, but the Stage is against him, as he cannot get one of his Plays acted. He got 60 Guineas for Taylor's Life.[9] I sent over your poetical Dictionary, which, I suppose, you have seen before this Time, and assure you it is in good Reputation, as you may judge, Mr. Johnson speaking very well of it. No one can tell who will be Lieutenant of Ireland. Covent Garden gets Money by the overflowing of Drury Lane. I had no Paper enclosed in your Letter of the 31st. Pray stay in Ireland until my Return, which will be early in March. I hope, as I propose, God willing to set out for that Country next Week, although the Number of my Acquaintance daily multiply. I wish you every Happiness, and am with best Wishes and Compliments to all Friends. Your most obedient and humble Servant.

George Faulkner

1. Ralph Verney, Earl Verney and Viscount Fermanagh in the Irish Peerage.
2. See Lecky, *A History of Ireland*, 2:60–62. Since 1495 "Poyning's Law," named after Sir Edward Poyning, Lord Lieutenant at the time, bound the Irish to accept and obey every law passed in England. Thus the Irish Parliament was unable to originate legislation except on the death of a king, after which action they could initiate a money bill as a free grant to the new king. The Irish Parliament refused to do so on the ascension to the throne of George III.
3. Both Carpenter and Brennan are unidentified.
4. Gilbert, "Streets of Dublin," p. 52. Peter Wilson, Dublin bookseller and printer. His *Dublin Magazine* was one of the first literary magazines (1762–1764). He also published the first city directory from 1752 to 1801.
5. Faulkner would appear to be at the Bedford or at a private lodging nearby.
6. Sir John Fielding; Arthur Murphy; George Coleman, the elder; Anthony Champion (1725–1801), poet and member of Parliament; either Robert Lloyd (1733–1764), poet and editor, or Rev. Evan Lloyd;

Thomas Wilson (1726–1799), D.D., professor of natural philosophy (1769) at Trinity College, Dublin, and classmate of Oliver Goldsmith.
7. Unidentifiable.
8. John Douglas (1721), D.D., divine and writer. Exposed Lauder's claim that Milton was a plagiarist.
9. There appears to be no factual basis for this.

George Faulkner to Samuel Derrick
(Forster 146, 50)

Dublin [sic], May 14, 1761

Dear Sir

I ought to have acknowledged the Favour of your last before more Time, but that I have been in Weekly Expectation of seeing you, and although I begin my Journey tomorrow for Dublin, yet I would not omit writing to you. I often see Lord Southwell, Mr. Mallet, Dr. Smollet, who all make friendly enquiry after you and last Week I dined with the last Gentleman at Salter's at Chelsea in a very agreeable Sett of Company: The Doctor proposeth going to Ireland next Summer, and to spend a Year or two in that Country, in Order to enable him the better to write that History.[1] Mrs. Sheridan is much pleased and obliged to you for sending the good Opinion you have of Sidney Bidulph.[2] Victor's Account of the Stage hath as good Reputation here as in Dublin.[3] Your Friend Murphy hath a Budget full of new Plays for the ensuing Season, which your Acquaintance Jones telleth me surpass all his others. I hear the Act for limiting the Number of Playhouses in London will be repealed next Session of Parliament for the Encouragement of Authors.[4] Harry Clark took the Extract of your Letter for Mrs. Ryan.[5] My Spirits are all in Hurry and Flutter preparing for my Journey so that I must conclude most cordially and affectionately your most humble Servant.

George Faulkner

1. See Knapp, *Tobias Smollett*, pp. 243 ff. Lewis Knapp hypothesizes that there was a distinct possibility that Smollett did come to

73

Ireland in the summer of 1761. There is nothing to contradict Smollett's statement that he would go to Ireland even though there is little factual evidence on how he traveled or where he traveled during that time.

2. [Mrs. Frances Sheridan], *Memoirs of Miss Sidney Bidulph, Extracted from Her Own Journal, and Now First Published.* Vol. 1 (Dublin: Printed by and for G. Faulkner, 1761).

3. *The History of the Theatres of London and Dublin from the Year 1730 to the Present* by Benjamin Victor. Faulkner advertised this for sale in his *Dublin Journal*, 30 May–2 June 1761.

4. *London Stage, 1660–1680,* 2, Pt. 4:807 ff. Faulkner, no doubt, heard the rumor which stemmed from an article in the *London Public Ledger* (21 March 1761). It stated that "leave will be applied for to the highest powers for a third Theatre in this City; and it is even hinted, that two well known actors have already ventured on a purchase, and are selecting a company with that design." Also Faulkner must have heard that Charles Reinhold, the singer, and Caudry, the actor, had previously applied for the summer patent for the Haymarket Theatre of Samuel Foote and his partner, Arthur Murphy. Thus Murphy and Foote were forced to rent Drury Lane for June, July, and August.

5. Unidentified.

George Faulkner to Samuel Derrick
(Forster 146, 51)

Dublin, Feb. 25, 1766

Dear Sir

After your very long Silence, it gave me the greatest Pleasure, as it always doth, to be favoured with a Letter from you. Sam. Smith[1] was paid the four Guineas you sent him, which I gave him the same Day that I got them from Mr. Loftus;[2] and, upon my speaking to Smith, he told me that he wrote the Letters to you, wherein he acknowledged the Receipt of the four Guineas.—We have had a most quiet Session of Parliament without any Riots or Tumult, nor was Dr. L. ever sent to Newgate or even ordered into Custody; but your London Newsprinters are always publishing cursed Lyes and improbable Falsehoods, of Ireland for which they have not the least Foundation. As to your Disputes in England about the Stamps and Taxes in America, I am very sorry for them–I had always looked upon the English as the most ignorant Politicians in the World. They might have been the greatest Nation that ever existed, had it not been for their Hatred and Severity to Ireland in cramping the Trade and Industry thereof, and for their stupid, ruinous, Continental Connections, which must end in the inevitable Ruin of England–Agreeable to your Desire I have drawn upon you in Favour of Mr. Lacey Hawes,[3] Bookseller, in London for six Guineas. I thank you for your Parliamentary Intelligence, and other news. We have little Wit or Politics here at present. Both our Theatres continue to oppose each other, by which they must be sufferers.

Tanduci and the other Italians are much liked, being very obliging. All my Family join with me, in the best Wishes and Compliments to you; and I am, Sir, your Majesty's

Most dutiful Subject, Most obedient
and most humble Servant,

George Faulkner

1. Sam. Smith would appear to be a second nephew to Faulkner as well as a journeyman printer who had special privileges in Faulkner's shop. Plomer et al., *Dictionary of Printers and Booksellers at Work in England, Scotland and Ireland, 1726–1757*, p. 427, lists him at work from 1759 to 1767. The columns of the *Dublin Journal* list him from 1759 to 1762 as "S. Smith at Mr. Faulkner's in Essex-street," and after 1765 as "S. Smith at Mr. Faulkner's in Parliament-street."

2. No positive identification. The man could be the Reverend Smythe Loftus, correspondent of Samuel Richardson and other English literary figures.

3. Lacy Hawes, London bookseller, held a part of the London copyright for the Swift *Works* with Charles Davis, Charles Hitch, the Dodsleys, and Bowyer.

———

CHARLES O'CONOR TO GEORGE FAULKNER § GEORGE FAULKNER TO CHARLES O'CONOR § The friendship between George Faulkner

(Protestant) and Charles O'Conor (Roman Catholic) of Bela-nagare (1710–1791) was not indicative of the times in which they lived. Yet their relationship points up the strength of character of both; each could overcome religious and political antipathies of the times and become close friend and correspondent.

Charles O'Conor was a Catholic country squire from Bela-nagare, County Roscommon. Faulkner, in all probability had known O'Conor before 1751 when he published O'Conor's pamphlet *Seasonable Thoughts on Our Civil Constitution.* Through Faulkner's help, O'Conor published several other pamphlets for loosening the strict anti-Catholic laws. O'Conor met influential Protestant churchmen and politicians at Faulk-ner's dinners and helped to create better rapport between the two religious groups.

Charles O'Conor to George Faulkner[1]
(British Museum, London, Egerton 201, f-31)

Belanagare, May 4. 1757.

I heartily congratulate with you, Dear Sir, on your safe Arrival in a Country to which you have rendered more Ser-vice than any other public or private Writer for several years past. The Hints you give, and the Truths you press, are, I think, preferable to Essays which fall but into few Hands, and become profitable in fewer. It was an Observation of our Patriot Dean (your particular Friend) that Plans of Refor-mation from without Doors were seldom considered *within.* The Rule is, I believe just, but several of his own Works might be argued as an Exception: yours must be excepted also, as well from the Manner in which they are conveyed as from the very extensive Circulation they meet with above all others. It is the more incumbent on you to go on, and goad a listless People into some Feeling. Their present helpless con-dition must surely come to your Aid.

But how shall I acknowledge your Obligations on myself in particular? You before brought me acquainted with the Bishop of Clogher.[2] You now bring Mr. Johnson and me to-gether.[3] In regard to the Prelate I willingly take an Opportunity of professing before you the Obligations I owe to him. He is possessed of great Talents improved by great literary Knowledge; but independent of both he is possessed of one talent superior to any Man I ever knew or read of; not excepting M. Bayle himself. The Nature of his Works exposed him to Opposition from Friends and Foes. But this he bore with an Elevation of Mind which neither the Selfishness of Erudition nor the Peevishness of Controversy could ever once ruffle. In his Replications (which are but few) he shews a proper Sensibility, but he shews it with Dignity. Malignity and Envy – Self-tormenting as they are, derive, however, some Pleasure from the Vexation they but too often give: My Lord of Clogher deprived them even of this.

I say nothing of Mr. Johnson. His Ramblers and other Works have set him (as Mr. Pope expresses it) *"at the Top of the Sublime Character."* As a Communication with such Men collects the most pleasing Circumstances of private Life, how much must I not owe to one who brought about such a Communication in my own Favour? I set this on the Level with the greatest Services ever done me.

I shall beg Leave, Dear Sir, to trouble you soon with forwarding a Letter from me to Mr. Johnson.[4] I am this Day too much taken up with the Thoughts of my own good Fortune not to communicate them to my Dublin Friends; Pride has a share in this, Mr. Faulkner's unmerited Service a greater.

I have no News for you; it is none I believe to inform you that this and the Northern Province are both undone. Here in particular we had great Loss of Sheep, and the frightful Seasons which surround us positively threaten a still greater loss of Human Creatures. I think such an event to be inevitable. Meal is come to three Shillings a Stone, and probably it will not admit of higher Price, as the Poor have nothing to give for it. Let it stand as an Aggravation of our Punishment, that we have as good arable Lands here as any in the Three Kingdoms. But the Roman Catholics live everywhere and have wasted all the Lands they could lay hold on, to carry on the useful Business of Pasturage: that alone enables them to pay their Rents and that furnishes the Landlord with the Means of importing hither the Wines of France. But the

Occupation of Pasturage has spread itself over all the Provinces: and thus it is with us, after a proper State of Reprise from the Year 1691 to this Day!

I hope your Travels have contributed to your Health. I am greatly interested in it, and I would request that you release yourself from Confinement often by taking the Air in an open Chair down to Clontarfe. I am with Gratitude, Esteem, and Affection

Sir,

Your most obliged and most willing Servant

Charles O'Conor

1. Portions of O'Conor's letters to Faulkner for 10 May and 25 May appeared in Charles O'Connor's article, "George Faulkner and the Irish Catholics," p. 492. The full text of the letters appears here for the first time.

2. See O'Connor, "George Faulkner and the Irish Catholics," p. 491; see also Gilbert, "Correspondence and Mss of Charles O'Conor," *Appendix to the Eighth Report*, Historical Documents Commission, 7:450. Faulkner introduced O'Conor to Bishop Clayton in 1755 in the hope of dissuading Clayton from further pushing of a Catholic Registry bill in the Irish Parliament. Both the friendship and the bill failed.

3. Faulkner sent Samuel Johnson a copy of O'Conor's 1753 edition of the *Dissertations on the History of Ireland*. See Boswell's *Life of Johnson*, 1:320.

4. Faulkner perhaps purposefully misunderstood Johnson's interest in the plight of the Roman Catholics. O'Conor as representative of the Catholic interest offered Johnson fifty guineas to write several pamphlets in behalf of the Irish Catholic cause. Johnson's attitude toward this proposal is unknown. Any correspondence between Faulkner and Johnson is lost. Boswell prints two letters from O'Conor to Johnson–twenty years apart. See Boswell, *Life of Johnson*, 1:320; 3:111.

Charles O'Conor to George Faulkner

(*Egerton 201, f–33*)

Belanagare, May 10. 1757.

Dear Sir

Enclosed I send you a Letter to be forwarded to Mr. Johnson. From these Contents, you must surely judge that

78

I am myself in earnest turned *Rambler*; I request you will make my Apology to him on this Account; I will engage him in the Cause of an innocent People, punished by Law for no other Reason but because they are mistrusted by the Law-makers. Your Engagements with the Public brought you acquainted with the Chief Men of this Party. And you can not think so meanly of their Honour and Gratitude but that they are as willing as able to make Mr. J. a suitable Return, could he be prevailed upon to undertake the Service of the Public so far as it can be connected with their Manumission from Bondage. You who acquired so much Popularity by weekly Paragraphs in Favour of the national Interest, and who have spread your Influence by keeping clear of Party Reflexions, are the fittest Man I know to negotiate this Affair sensibly with our People. Dr. Jennings will assist you with his own Interest among them, and I need not mention many more to you who certainly will be far from putting the least Slight on a Project which, if brought to bear (with your Friend beyond the Water) is indisputably the best laid which could be thought on for restoring us all to that Condition in which King William wisely left us. I shall dun and solicit my Friends in the City on this Subject, as soon as you give me Leave. I am in the meantime with the greatest Affection and Gratitude.

Your most obliged and obedient Servant
Charles O'Conor

Charles O'Conor to George Faulkner
(Egerton 201, f-35)

Belanagare May. 25. 1757

Dear Sir,

After my Return from Coloony in the County of Sligoe, I found your Letter of the 14th Inst. here, and I know not which to admire most, the public or private Benevolences which it reconciles and displays. You have shewn that the least popular of those Endowments, is not the least amiable; and without refining much on the Matter I think it might be shewn from the Instancies afforded by you and a few others that the strongest Pretensions to the one are best supported by a constant Exertion of the other. I have a Right to tell you this, because you have enriched me both ways. And I would rather fail in Delicacy towards you, than in this Duty of Acknowledgement, which it would be a Crime in me to omit, and which, in Truth, my moral Essence would not bear omitting.–The Book you sent me from Dr. *Brown*[1] is one of those Performances which come out but very rarely, and which if the Public knows not how to *Estimate*, one Argument more can be subjoyned *to his*, of the Reality of those impending Evils, which is much easier to prophesy than to remedy, to explain than to prevent. He here traced it and cites its Cause with a Penetration and Precision that failed all the Writers before him on this Subject; at least I think so: But his leaving our Reformation at the Mercy of a *Power of Necessity* drawn from the Vices, not the Virtues of the People, is a tremendous Conclusion! May we not hope that his and others opening our Eyes at the Brink of the Precipice [crossed out] must supersede the Evil he threatens? It is his Business as a Preacher and a Prophet to put the hardest Features into the Picture of Vice; Tho Deformity may have a good Effect, and *that* Effect may shew that we are not as far gone in Rapacity, Fashion and want of Virtue as he represents. We may be allowed to endulge such a Thought to a certain Degree; To flatter ourselves *with it*, would I fear be fatal. You are a very extraordinary Man; It is not enough that you should make me a Reader for 25 Years past, but you should also at this Time make me a Author-Husbandman in one Species of Industry unknown to any of my Neighbors. Is it not a Shame that a perpetual Citizen should have it so much in his Power to instruct us in our own Trade? But however that be, it is a Maxim with us Tillers of the Soil to receive Instruction very gratefully from every Quarter, and I hope in a short Time to make the Faulkner *Turnip*[2] as generally known in this Country as the *Croston Apple*, which yields our best Cyder. My learned and excellent Friend Dr. Jennings will I know, to his utmost, exert himself in the Affair which, I trust, you will be enabled to negotiate with Mr. J——n.[3] You happily opened and you have been long opening, a Treaty of Peace between the Public and the Party hitherto very obnoxious on the Score of Religion. It is our Business to pursue with great Earnestness such a Treaty, if possible, to its Conclusion. If we fail, we shall fail with Honour, at least with a better Impression than any which Zeal could hitherto give or Prejudice receive; And is not that gaining a great Point? Materials from Acts of Parliament and from Reason previous and often superior to all Acts of popular Assemblies shall not be wanting to your Friend if he can be won to act in this one Capacity for the Public, and (may I say) for his own Fame. My Cousin Reilly of Usher's Street (the Editor of the Dissertations) will supply a good part of those Materials, if you or Dr. Jennings apply to him. I have been out all this Day attending Pioneers enclosing one of my Parks. I shall however write another Letter this Night if I can to Dr. Jennings. If I can not, I request you will apologize for me, till I can more fully give him my Mind by the next Post. I hope I need not tell you that I am with equal Gratitude and Affection.

Sir
Your most obliged and most
obedient Servant
Charles O'Conor

1. John Brown (1715-1766), Whig preacher, playwright, and essayist. The book Faulkner sent O'Conor was Brown's best known work, *An Estimate of the Manners and the Principles of the Times.* Faulkner advertised this book for sale in his *Dublin Journal,* 14-17 May 1757.

2. While one cannot quite recover the joke, there is a clear reference to the work of "Turnip" Townshend (Charles, Second Viscount). See Pope, *Imitations of Horace,* II, ii, 273.

3. Johnson.

Charles O'Conor to George Faulkner
(Egerton 201, f-37)

Feb. 15. 1762

Dear Sir

Since I had the Pleasure of waiting last of yours, I had the ill Luck of spraining my ankle on the Stairs of Dick's Coffee House,[1] what confined me to my Apartment all this Time. I am now I thank God tolerably well and will be soon able to thank you in Person for the many Acts of Friendship. As I have not an domestick Frank I request you will forward the enclosed to Dr. Warner.[2] I am with great Affection and Gratitude

Dear Sir
Your very obedient Serv't.
C. O'Conor

1. Gilbert, "Streets of Dublin," p. 594. "Like most of the other coffee houses in Dublin, Dick's was located on the drawingroom floor, one of the shops underneath being occupied by Thomas Cotter, bookseller and publisher, and another by the 'Hoop' eating house."
2. Fernando Warner (1703–1768), D.D., rector of Barnes, Surrey. He wrote a one volume history of Ireland and a history of the English church.

Charles O'Conor to George Faulkner
(Egerton 201, f-39)

Mar. 17. 1762

Dear Sir

My Sickness and my Avocations since my Recovery deprived me of the Pleasure of waiting on you all this Time. But I shall soon have the Gratification. Mean Time I send you for Your Curiosity a printed Letter of Dr. Warner's to Lord Littleton.[1] This with other Letters for myself I rec'd two Days since, from Belanagare, being directed thither from Barnes on the Presumption that I was at home. The Doctor requires answers from me to several Observations Ld. Littleton made to passages in the Dissertations, you put into the Doctor's Hands.[2] When I have a Minute of Leisure, I will employ it in an Endeavour to satisfy these Gentlemen, and I think I can not do it more effectually than by giving up some few Things in favor of the rest as we preserve a physical Body by the Amputation of parts which might in time mortify the Whole. I am (my Dear Sir) with great affection and Gratitude

Your very obed't Servt.
C. O'Connor [sic][3]

1. George Lyttleton (1709-1773), first Baron Lyttleton. His *History of the Life of Henry II and the Times He Lived In* was a lifetime work.
2. O'Conor's *Dissertations on the History of Ireland*.
3. The manuscript is corrupt and the misspelling of O'Conor's name is a doubtful reading of the signature.

Charles O'Conor to George Faulkner

(Egerton 201, f-41)

Belanagare Aug. 8. 1763

Dear Sir

After my Return from the County of Sligo I found your very obliging and friendly Letter of the 26 past. Nay, I found more of your Presents spread before Me: Dr. Herring's[1] *Sermons* and the Duke of Leeds's *Thoughts* on a Bill he debated in the House of Lords of England toward the Close of the last Century.[2] The Nobleman's Discourse equally supported by Eloquence and Argument was the more welcome to see as it characterizes the Times, and forms a curious historical Anecdote, which must be preserved. The Prelate's Sermons I have read throughout. No man was happier in a clear unaffected Expression, and you have certainly put your Finger on the best Discourse in the whole Collection the Fourth Sermon: Universal Charity was never better explained in that Discourse that concludes happily by a fine Quotation of a favourite Author of mine, the Abbe Fleury,[3] a Man of Doctor Herring's own Temper, equally an Enemy to Persecution and Superstition. I had, I confess strong Prejudices against Dr. Herring from the Character given of him in your Edition of Dr. Swift's Works, Vol. 1, p. 283.[4] Dr. Swift was little inclined to think favourably of Court Chaplains and in Dr. Herring's Case might be easily misinformed.

You are well known through these Kingdoms for one who never put a Slight on any Scheme which might derive Honour and consequently Advantage to your native Country. You have happily succeeded in many. You have enriched us with good Books and you have from Week to Week been active in throwing out Hints for the Consideration of Men in Power which have been improved to national Advantage, but which might otherwise be most certainly overlooked, but for your weekly Admonitions and repeated Solicitations. After all, I need not read that your Passion to see your Country distinguished and consequently benefited by a good History, can not be gratified. The Scheme that I laid before Dr. Sullivan would be considered in every Country in Europe but our own.[5] Other Thoughts engross the Attention of our Men of Rank; and we may compound for the Oblivion of all our former Actors on this Stage so that their own Conduct furnishes better Materials for the future History of it. "Should the Case prove otherwise," future History will do Mr. Faulkner Justice. His Activity in the public Service will be remembered as well as the Deeds of those who declined (on the Score of private Considerations) to cooperate with him. I render you warm Thanks for your Intention to send me the Geohegan's Book,[6] and I am glad that so judicious an Historian as Dr. Leland[7] approves of it. I expect in a few days his three volumes on high Affairs. My Correspondent in France having told he remitted them to Mr. Anthony Dermot for my Wife.

I had last Week a Letter from Dr. Warner full of Complaints of the Slight put upon him by our Countrymen. A certain great Man called for three Copies, another for only one of his History: Smollet in the *Critical Review*[8] treated him with Disingenuity and Malice and Mr. Wilson of Dame-street is going on (he says) with a piratical edition to his Detriment; nay, he is displeased with you for detecting a Mistake of his, as he thinks it of little Consequence and he insists on the Propriety of calling Ireland a *Province*, not an Imperial Kingdom, as it was denominated in the Council of Constance. To a Man whose Heart was so full, I did not think it proper for me to heighten his Concern by pointing out several Mistakes of his in matter of Fact. I told him in general Terms, that he was mixed in some Accounts by Keating, who ought not to be trusted in a single line, where he may not be supported by our old Annals.

I am much obliged to Mr. Howard[9] for thinking so fa-vourably of me, and to you for writing me his Sentiments. While two such men think well of my Endeavours, and Studies, I take it that I have Encouragement enough to pro-ceed. To be useful to the Public may not be in our Power, to labour to be so is doubly our Duty.

I am with great Gratitude and Affection, dear Sir,

Your most obliged and obedient Servant

Charles O'Conor

1. Thomas Herring (1690–1757), D.D., court chaplain and later Archbishop of Canterbury (1747–1757). Satirized by Swift.
2. The pamphlet is not readily identifiable. The British Museum Catalogue lists a pamphlet, *The Late Duke of Leeds's Reasons for Pro-testing Against a Vote Made in the House of Lords in England which Declared a Certain Tryal before the House of Lords of Ireland to be Coram non Judice*, which might be a reprint of the pamphlet.
3. Abbé Fleury (1640–1723), religious writer. He wrote discourses on Plato and *History of the French Laws*.
4. See Swift, *Works*, 12:36. The *Intelligencer* Papers, vol. 3: "But I should be very sorry that any of them should be so weak, as to imitate a *Court Chaplain* in England, who preached against the *Beggar's Opera;* which will probably do more Good than a thousand sermons of so stupid, so injudicious and so prostitute a Divine."
5. Gilbert, "Correspondence and Mss of Charles O'Conor," *Ap-pendix to the Eighth Report*, 7:486, describes a proposal which O'Con-or made to Francis Stoughton Sullivan, professor of Feudal and English

Law concerning the publication of a Gaelic manuscript *The Annals of the Four Masters.* Sullivan was not interested.

6. James MacGeoghegan (1702–1763), an Irish abbot living in France. His *Histoire de L'Irland* appeared in 1758. Volumes two and three appeared in 1762 and 1763 respectively. See also Gilbert, "Correspondence and Mss of Charles O'Conor," *Appendix to the Eighth Report*, 7:463.

7. Thomas Leland (1722–1785), D.D., Senior Fellow and Latin Scholar at Trinity College, Dublin.

8. Tobias Smollet, "Review of *The History of Ireland*": "To do the doctor justice, however, his narratives and apologies are sometimes not destitute of plausibility, though they always are of historical precision; and his stile and manner are such, as much delight those readers who are fond of that species of writing which we may call historical romance, or rather, spectral history: for we must again repeat it, that many of the doctor's spectres are the resemblances of beings who were once certainly clothed with flesh and blood; and a man of erudition and genius may very possibly still from the names of places, the traditions of the natives, and the faint remains of antiquity, compose a very curious dissertation upon the reality of such existences, tho' such a work would feed rather the rich than the purposes of knowledge."

9. Gorges Edmond Howard (1715–1786), author and lawyer.

Charles O'Conor to George Faulkner
(Egerton 201, f-43)

Dublin, Sept. 25 1766[1]

Dear Sir

I have been here for some time and am now returning to Connaught. All my public News you know better than we do, and yet we know more than enough, of your political Warfare in England. It is indeed amazing to us at this Distance, that an Administration which gave the Public no Provocation, should be attacked with a Fury and Illiberality unworthy of so wise and great a People as you live with; and we can not but think that the winter Campaign in St. Stephen's Chapel will be managed with a Decency and Temper more reputable to the National Character.—Private News such as may be pleasing to you, I throw upon Paper just as it offers—I dined lately in Parliament Street with your Nephew. You are happy

in their Care and Conduct, and you can remain the longer
where you are, from the Conviction that your Absence will
not prove detrimental to your domestic Affairs. Where you
are, you can enjoy many of those who loved you at Home,
and have been happy under your Roof; and if you have any
Anxiety, it must only regard your Separation from the
Friends you left behind you. I dined this last week with Dr.
Leland, and viewed with Pleasure in his dining Room as fine
a Portrait of you as Hands could draw. He is a very learned,
and what is infinitely better, a very worthy Man. He is one
of the Friends you gave me, one of the Number who do
Honour to this Country by their Ability as well as Rank:
Men of liberal and national Endowments, who have thrown
away the Weeds of spiritual Hatred, together with the Jeal-
ousies and Mistrusts which stick to the Soil. They may do
Good, or if they can not, they will teach their Posterity to do
it. To unite all Parties in these Kingdoms in one Creed of
Civil Faith is possible, nay very practicable, and it were to be
wished that those who oppose such an Union in Civil Ortho-
doxy, assigned any one Instance wherein it could be hurtful
to Britain or Ireland–Poor Lord Taaffe one of your Friends,
left us last Sunday and is now in London in his way to Germany. He drew up here, *Some Observations on Affairs in
Ireland from 1691 to the Present Time.*[2] He employed a
Friend[3] to digest the Materials and throw them into the Present Form: The Whole was indeed executed from too short a
Notice of his Lordship's Intention, as is evident from Inac-
curacies and some other Marks of Hurry in the Work. The
Main of the Argument however is (I think) well supported–
"This, says his Lordship, is the best Legacy I can leave behind
me, and the only Service, which the established Laws permit
me to render my Native Country, Let it remain as a Pledge
of Affection I owe to my King, to my Country, and to the
present free Constitution of our Government, and let me
flatter myself that I may still be useful, *if the Time is come*,
as I trust it is, when useful Information may dare encounter
every favorite Error etc." But enough of this. I now live in
my Son's House in Anderson's Court, Cow-lane.
    Next Day–after Mr. Burke of Wendover[4] landed here,

he paid me a Visit in this Retreat and I shall retain a grateful Memory of his several Acts of Friendship. He has retired into the Country to philosophize on the present Storms of State, remote from all Danger. When fair Weather is made for the Administration, he will shine again for the Good of these Kingdoms. Such Talents and such Patience of Temper as he proposes must doubtless produce Good. How is my Friend Miss Smith?[5] You did well to make her the Companion of your Travels. So sensible a young Gentlewoman so nearly connected with you by Affection as well as Blood, will remove every Heaviness of a vacant Hour from you; and as Nature has given you a very sound Constitution, she will be free from the Pain she would otherwise suffer, from any Failure in your Health: I have nothing to add, but that, in General, all your Friends here long for you, and that in particular, I long to hear of your Welfare. It would be a particular Favour if you gave me Satisfaction on this Subject and whether you direct hither or to Belanagare your Letter will find me and be a most hospitable Present to

Dear Sir
your most obliged and obedient Servant
Charles O'Conor

1. O'Conor's letter to Faulkner finds him in London, possibly at the Bedford Coffee House.

2. Nicholas, Lord Viscount Taafe was one of six Catholic peers of Ireland. His *Observations on Affairs in Ireland from the Settlement in 1691 to the Present Time* created a paper war when it was published in 1767.

3. Gilbert, "Correspondence and Mss of Charles O'Conor," *Appendix to the Eighth Report*, 7:452ff. The friend is O'Conor. O'Conor, at Taafe's request, prepared a statement for him on the case of the Irish Catholics in Ireland.

4. Edmund Burke.

5. Miss Smith is Faulkner's niece, probably the sister of the previously mentioned Sam Smith. Another niece of Faulkner is seldom mentioned. W. P. Courtenay in his article "Lord Halifax-Dunk," *Dictionary of National Biography*, 15:291, states that a niece and later adopted daughter, Mary Anne Faulkner, was the mistress of Halifax when he came to Ireland as Lord Lieutenant October 1761.

Charles O'Conor to George Faulkner

(*Egerton 201, f-45*)

Belanagare Oct. 28 1766

Dear Sir

Having been lately in Dublin, I laid hold of the Opportunity, to pursue you to London, in a Letter; and yet before I would come up with you, on the Wings of Paper; you were, I doubt, at that very time, out of my reach at Bath. Indeed I had little to communicate to you besides Expressions of my own Gratitude for your repeated Acts of Friendship. If I am good for anything, it is for my Sensibility to good Offices, and when I reflect on the Friends you gave me, (Lord Aran,[1] Lord Moira,[2] Judge Marshal,[3] Dr. Leland, the Dean of Down,[4] etc.) I feel how much more I owe you than to the rest of Mankind. I can not make you a better Return, than by availing myself of the Advantages of such Friendships, and to guard against the Indiscretions by which they may be lost. I shall have no Difficulty, I thank God, in acting so prudent a Part; and I often thought in a Country so shamefully, and indeed so fatally, rent by religious Aversons, nothing could be more desirable than what has actually come to pass: The Interposition of a Citizen under whose Root all Parties are brought together, and from whence they retired, with the happy Disappointment of being pleased with one another. The human Mind is never happier than in the Discovery of Mistakes, which increases its Benevolence, and it is to the want of a Center of Communication, such as you have fixed, that such Discoveries are not made. Without it we are shy of meeting together, nay, as things are, unhappily circumstanced, can not meet.

You see then, what Merit you have with the Public, by teaching us, as Lord Shaftsbury finely phrases it "to rub off our course Corners by an amicable Collision."[5] Nature gave you an excellent Constitution, and it is happy for you, that Hospitality has not hitherto preyed upon it: Years, however, will make Entertainments and Parties impossible. Such Encroachments may be, in your Case, yet you will foresee the

Necessity of setting their Consequences at a Distance, by less Indulgence at your Table, and I may say, less frequent Calls of your Friends about you. I would have you live long; your Country is interested in your doing so, and Nature has given you a good long Tether, which you must take care not to cut short.

I am now, I thank God, sound in my Feet, and have no Complaints relatively to physical Evil. Through Dr. Leland's Friendship I can now have Access to the College Manuscripts, notwithstanding the Strictness of their university Statutes. I amuse myself in the Business of an Irish Antiquarian; and I am pained at being alone in such an Occupation; none to improve by, none to instruct me! To mend the Matter, the very Subject is despised, and I am too far gone in Years to make any considerable Acquisition, or stem the Torrent of Discouragement. I have no more to do, than to suit my Ends to the Means.

You are just arrived from England "laden (said Vergil to Augustus) with the *Spoils of the East*." When therefore you have a vacant Hour, I request you will unload a part of your Treasure at my Door, in a few Lines on Paper. Your Letter left at my Son's House in Anderson's Court Cow-lane will be safely conveyed to me. Meantime, you will be so kind to tender my Affections to your whole Family, to worthy Leland, Captain Desbrusay,[6] and our other common Friends. I am unalterably

Dear Sir,
Your most obliged and obedient Servant
Charles O'Conor

1. Sir Arthur Gore, created Earl of Arran in 1758.
2. Sir John Rawdon, first Earl of Moira.
3. Robert Marshall, judge in the Irish Court of Common Pleas.
4. Patrick Delany (1685–1768).
5. Anthony Ashley Cooper, Third Earl of Shaftsbury, *Characteristics of Men, Manners, Opinions, and Times*, 1:46. "All politeness is owing to Liberty. We polish one another, and rub off our corners and rough sides by a sort of amicable collision."
6. See "Affairs of Her Majesty's Land Forces," *Gentleman's Magazine* 31 (1761): 612. Theophilus Debrusay, Dublin commissary agent for the British Army establishment.

Charles O'Conor to George Faulkner
(Egerton 201, f–47)

Belanagare June 13. 1767

Dear Sir

I take sensible Pleasure in acknowledging my many obligations to you: and yet, I would not bring my Gratitude under any Suspicion by the too frequent, or too indiscreet Declarations of what I owe you; at least, if I erred in this particular, it would be towards yourself; for awhile I kept clear of all affectation, it could surely be no Error to tell my Friends (as frequently as it comes my Way) that I am greatly in your Debt; I do so, and for want of better payments, I return you my sincere Affections. Happily, I am one of the Number, on whom your Services have not been thrown away, and I would not exchange the Pleasure I derive from the grateful Turn of my Temper, for any Condition on Earth drawn from Treachery and Ingratitude. This Reflexion reminds me of the Number of worthy Men you introduced me to, some of Rank in public Life, others in Literature; and such Men I shall retain (with God's Favor) in such a Manner, as will not put your Friendship[1] to the blush. I certainly will offend none, and it is well to deserve this negative Merit, if I can have no other with them. Dr. Leland's Friendship I shall never forget, for it came recommended with an Openness and Candor which lays his Heart bare and lets the Person he gives it to, see at once the Value of the Acquisition he makes. I am in great Pain for him, and request you will take me out of it, by giving me an Account that he is now on his Leggs. Thru' his Kindness I was made free of the College Library, and I am extreamly thankful to Dr. Andrews[2] for his Civility during the ten Days that I have been perusing the Irish Annals thro'[3] the Reigns of the Plantagents and Tudors. In fact, the History of our own Country from the Time of Henry 2 to the late Revolution is to that of the present Age, the most important: an able Man would instruct Mankind by a Recital of it, and Materials are not wanting. It is a post of Literature not yet (to our Shame) occupied by any Writer that deserves the Name. Dr. Leland would fill such a post with Dignity. He would[4] thro' his Philosophical Knowledge render us wiser than we are, and no Nation ever wanted the true Knowledge of their proper Interests more than ours. History in such Hands[5] would reform us much. Would to God he could be brought to think of this Matter, this Duty I should say which he owes to his Country. I should in such a Case tho' in the Decline of Life, sit down for Months to translate the Irish Annals for him, and I think he would find some useful Matter in the Rubbish that I should throw out to him. But enough of this, 'til we hear of our Friend's Recovery. When he is well, you should urge him on this Head and let him feel the reproach, that if we do not exhibit a Hume or a Robertson in our own Island, it will be his Fault.

I request you will give my Affection to Miss Smith and Nephews. You'll please also to tender my Services to my Brother Milesian, Mr. Sheridan and the other Friends you gave me, etc.

On the presumption that I was still in Town, the Librarian of St. Sepulchre's sent a polite Card to my Son's House requiring a copy from me of the *Dissertations;* It was, I confess, an oversight in me, that I have not anticipated that Requisition, by lodging a Copy in that Library. I request you will make my Apology to the Library Keeper and send him a Copy, for which I shall be accountable to you 4d. as soon as I go up to Town.

When you are at Leisure nothing could be more gratifying to me than a Line from you. I am very truly

My Dear Sir
your most obliged and obed't Serv't.

C. O'Conor

1. Crossed out.
2. Francis Andrews (d. 1774), D.D., became Provost of Trinity College, Dublin, in 1758.
3. Crossed out.
4. Crossed out.
5. Crossed out.

Charles O'Conor to George Faulkner
(Egerton 201, f-49)

Belanagare July. 10. 1767

Dear Sir

After my Return from the County of Sligoe, I found your Letter of the 23rd of June[1] here before me. It gave me great Pleasure to find you as inflexible as ever in the Service of your Country; and it gave me great Pain, to find the Iniquity of the Dublin Pirates equally perseverant in robbing you.[2] Indeed they rob the Public in spite of all your Spirit, for how can you hold out under a Discouragement which from its Constancy is almost equal to a legal Prohibition? And might not all this excuse our People the Necessity of sending to England for well printed Books? By the way, I am amazed at the Supiness or Inattention of the reputable Gentlemen of your Profession, in not making an Application to Parliament for a Redress of a Grievance which affects the whole Public, as well as Individuals. Would not a Law to secure the Property of Publishers be most useful, would it not merit more Attention, than those Statutes which, have from Time to Time been created for Preserving our Grouce and Partridges? I say that the Inattention of fair Publishers, and of the Manufacturers of Paper and Types to this Point is amazing, and of none more than yourself, who have the Friendship and Interest of so many Members in both Houses, for procuring a Bill to remedy the Evil. I am not apt to overrate the Merit or Spirit of my Countrymen, and yet I think too well of them not to conclude; they will resent the Injury done you; in pirating a Book of which the Noble Author has made you sole Proprietor in this Kingdom. I thank you heartily for the Honour you extended me in believing I could furnish some marginal Notes relatively to that Part of Lord Lyttleton's History, which regards Ireland. A few such Notes, I confess could be supplied, for the second Volume of the Annals of the Four Masters now in the College Library, and I think his Lordship would not be offended at the Insertion; but, unluckily, I am not now in Dublin to sellect such particulars; If I was, no Person in the Kingdom would take greater pleasure in Rendering you that small Service than I; for I am so bound to you by Interest, that it can hardly give any Display to my Gratitude. If I could render you any Service where I am, it would be by submitting to your Consideration, whether you should not issue a Notice to the Public through the Channel of the *Journal* (a little Bill of Complaint) of Injury done you, this the Piracy of a Work of which the Noble Author made you sole Proprietor, etc. I am thinking that such a Notice would produce the proper Effect of leaving an ill printed and ill-corrected Book on the Hands of the Pirate.

You gave me self-interested, and indeed, national Pleasure in the Account you give me of Dr. Leland's Recovery. As a great Scholar, and what is much better, as a Philosopher, his Country has a Demand on his Abilities, and however the History of a Greek King[3] who flourished in a remote Antiquity has spread his Fame, yet the History of his own Country from the Time of Henry Second forward might, he must confess, be more useful to the Public of our own Kingdom, and I may even say, the Public of all Europe. Such a Man was born to moderate and repress the Civil, the religious and the shameful Prejudices which poison us as Individuals, and weaken us as Nations united under the same Government. Providence bestows such Abilities for the best of Purposes, and if the Possessors do not answer to the Designation, they are accountable, and I am afraid culpable.–Had I not this Affair greatly at Heart, I would not be so presumptuous as to offer my own Thoughts, even in a private Letter, and under such an Impulse (wherein I am acquitting myself of a Duty). I am confident both the Doctor and you will pardon me. I request you will present my Affections to your whole Family, and after wishing you Happiness and health to enjoy it,

I conclude
My dear Sir
Charles O'Conor

1. The letter is not extant.
2. Faulkner in his *Dublin Journal*, 17-20 June 1767, made known to

his readers his anger concerning the pirating of the second edition of *Universal History* in folio. The following advertisement could have been seen by O'Conor:

"To the Public.

George Faulkner having for many years past, at great Expence and Trouble, printed and published several Books and Pamphlets for the Service of his Country, by promoting Knowledge, encouraging the manufactures of Printing Types, Paper, Copperplates, and many other branches of Trade, thereby saving large Sums from being sent out of the Kingdom for the above Articles: yet such hath been the Malignity, Hatred, Envy and Malice of some insidious People of his Profession, that they have not only pyrated Books and Pamphlets upon him, to the Diminution of his Fortune, but injury of his Copies, all which he obtained in the fairest Manner from different Authors and Proprietors in Great Britain and Ireland, at much Trouble and Expence, in his Journies to and fro: And whereas other Booksellers have lately had many Pyracies committed on them, they, in conjunction with each other, to save themselves and Families from inevitable Ruin, have been obliged to sell their Books and Pamphlets at less Expence than Paper and Print, to their very great Loss: And whereas Books of great Value, particularly one Work, the largest ever undertaken by any Bookseller in Ireland, and printed on better Paper, Type and Copperplates than were ever known in this Kingdom, have been pyrated on George Faulkner. . . . Many and just have been the Complaints of Books and Pamphlets not being well printed in this Nation: And how can it be otherwise, when the most elegant Editions have been pyrated to the irreparable damage of the Proprietors, by which Authors, Printers, Booksellers, Bookbinders, Paper makers, Letterfounders, and many other People whose Livelihood depend thereon, must inevitably perish or quit the Kingdom, unless these wicked Practices can be prevented? Mr. Faulkner doth hereby call on all the Trade, to know if he ever offended one of them, or if he ever pyrated a Book, Play, Pamphlet or even a single Page or Line upon any of them. If he did not, why should they rob him?"

3. Gilbert, "Correspondence and Mss of Charles O'Conor," *Appendix to the Eighth Report*, 7:486, identifies this book as *The Life and Reign of Philip, King of Macedon*, 1758.

Charles O'Conor to George Faulkner

(Egerton 201, f-51)

Belanagare Sept. 4, 1767

Dear Sir

Your Letter and Pacquet of the First instant I rec'd last Night and I return you infinite Thanks for your frequent

Acts of Friendship. I am greater Gainer by them, and they are inhanced greatly to me, as I receive them, amidst so many Avocations of yours, public and personal. The 54 pages you sent me of Lord Lyttleton's History I read last Night and again this Morning with great Avidity nor did he disappoint my Expectations of him, as a fine Painter and a fair one also. Since that as far as I can judge or know (from what I saw) he does not draw from Prejudice or Affectation, but each Character sat for the Picture and whether good or bad his coloring is excellent, without Gaudiness or Quaintness.[1] I told you above I am a great Gainer by your Friendship, for you gave me many Friendships with it, and all the Return I can make you, is not to put you under any pain for giving them; I hope confidently that I have Discretion and Prudence enough to keep what I got, and, at worst, in the Negative good Quality of giving no Offense. But I am, I know, a Loser by not being oftener near you, and I am pained that I have not been lately so, as I should have seen Lord Clare whose Family and personal Abilities I am acquainted with. I am also a Loser by not knowing Count Serant personally. I am much pleased that O'Gorman made one in the Circle lately about your Table, and it gave me Pleasure [when] he and I dined with you (on the Blind Quay) that he rendered himself so agreeable to Lords Moira and Aran: we had indeed that Night a long Sitting but[2] a very pleasing one. Mr. O'Gorman was bred a Scholar and Phisician in the University of Paris and is better qualified to write the natural and civil History of the County of Clare (upon Smith's Plan[3]) for which he has collected the best Materials. He has a good Mind, which is better than all the Sciences, without Quality. My worthy and benificient Friend (one of the Friendships you gave me) Dr. Leland is mounted too high on the Steps of Fame; Does he not think, it would be descending, to write the History of his Native Country down from the Time of Henry 2? The History of Freebootery on the one side, and Savages (what Mr. Hume calls them) on the other? But this is grounded on a Mistake. We have not been much greater Savages and Free-booters than our Neighbours during the Feudal Ages; and the History of Man on every Stage is worthy of being known, tho' doubtless one Period rewards the pains of an able Historian[4] better than another; and yet, is nothing due to the Land of our Birth? Shall this, and this Island alone be a Blank in the History of Europe? Dr. Leland will let it be so, and let him be answerable for it. He knows well that I have not abilities for the Task[5] I would wish he undertook; If I had, he knows that in the Decline of Life I could do little and that little in the part of a Pioneer, to digg and throw up Materials for him, or such as him. I am luckily saved that Labor, and it may be happy for me as I am almost past my Labor. I make my Letter prolix because I love to be long in your Company, and yet the Desire has better Grounds than mere Selfishness upon such a Principle. Alone I should be contemptible in my own Idea. I am employed by Day in the Business of Agriculture, and by Night I converse with Philosophers, and (by way of Relaxation, or contrast) with Divines. In both I discern great Weakness as well as great Strength. If God grants Life I will next November change the Scene, and hive myself (like the Bees) during the bad Season in your Capitol. Meantime, I request you will tender my Affections to Miss Smith with whom I shall quarrel, if she does not change her Name before I see her. My best Services to my worthy young Friend Mr. Todd and Mr. Smith. I am (my Dear Sir)

Your most obig'd and obed't Serv't
C. O'Conor

1. Gilbert, "Correspondence and Mss of Charles O'Conor," *Appendix to the Eighth Report*, 7:487. O'Conor wrote a week later to Dr. Curry on the same subject. He stated that "This fortnight past I am reading Lord Lyttleton's 'History of Henry II,' sent to me in packets (franked by T. LeHunte) from my friend Mr. Sheriff Faulkner. I have yet received 270 pages. It is the work of an able, judicious, and critical writer; and yet, relatively to the ecclesiastical part of the history, he fills the character of a good Protestant than of a disengaged philosopher. How few even of the greatest men have elevation of mind enough to assert their natural freedom on such occasions! They talk much of liberty, and are themselves slaves of opinion."
2. Crossed out.
3. Crossed out.
4. Crossed out.
5. Crossed out.

Charles O'Conor to George Faulkner

(Egerton 201, f–53)

Belanagare. Sept. 15. 1767

Dear Sir

In one of the Six Pacquets I received from you last Thursday, I notice your most friendly Letter, and you have my perpetual Gratitude in Return. When you ventured on remitting, at once, such a large Cargo by one Post, it was judicious in you to procure the *Pass* of Mr. [Lehunte]; least the Post Officers should grow so suspicious of so bulky a Correspondence with a Papist. By the way, I am assured, that Mr. Lehunte is a humane and obliging Landlord to his own Popish tenants, and that he can reconcile two (seamingly) strange Extreams, *Hatred* to the Party and *good will* to the Individuals. Lord Lyttleton's History will do good, because it will make us wiser; and when we are a little wiser, we will, at worst, forbear and relent; if [we] do not reform.–This is gaining a great point, at a Time when gaining and (in Ireland particularly) was a happiness despaired of.–The Reproach against us, that our Historical Productions were not equal to those of the Continent, was I believe, just. That Reproach is now removed since Hume, Robertson and Lyttleton appeared; and [Mr.] Hume in one particular perhaps, excells all our ablest Historians, (as) he is not fettered by Principles, which tho' doubtless the best in [Honesty] yet produce the worst Effects when ill understood, and consequently, ill-applied. In Truth, such principles [crossed out–when] turned devious from their true Intention, make no sort of Difference between the Inquisitions of Spain and those of England. The *Matter* is the Same, the *form* different and we may thank our excellent political Constitution that [unreadable] struggles with the Disease and resists all its Violence. It will be visited with greater Force nay it may be shaken off, if such Men as Lord Lyttleton; (Men of Authority and Rank) continue to write: Writers in a Superior orb who do not permit Religious Zeal, to extinguish the Lights of Philosophy. I shall owe a great deal to Dr. Leland's Indulgence, if [he] forgives me the Warmth, with which I would fain turn his Talents to a more particular Application, relatively to (the) Interest and wants of his Countrymen. He too is a Philosopher, as well as a Christian; He has youth and strength, and will do good in whatever Subjects he writes upon. I request that you will present (him) the Friend you gave me with my Affections and Gratitude.

You have good, and, I think, effectual Interest with the Leading Men in both Houses of Parliament, and you [crossed out] will merit just Reproach if you do not push that Interest with them, to obtain a legal Remedy against the Robber of [your] and others property, [crossed out] relatively to the publication of good [books]. In other Countries the press is *restrained*, from doing Good; In Ireland it is *permitted* to do acknowledged Evil, even to the Public as well as to Individuals.

I wish I may hear from O'Gorman. You may sooner. If you do, be pleased to inform him that he is welcome to the use of my Ortelius, which I left with you for sometime with a View to draw in Subscriptions for his map of Ireland as it was [crossed out] inhabited in his time.

With the warmest Gratitude I accept of your Assistance in my Occupation as a Tiller of the Earth, and if you send DuHamil's Husbandry to my Son's house in Anderson's Court, Cow Lane, it will be safely convayed to me. I enjoy 800 Acres still of the old Family Estate, the Plank on which we came on Shore (as I told Judge Marshal at your Table) after our great ship-wreck. You will enable me to reclaim the additional 300 Acres which are [crossed out] yet worth nothing. Mean time I thank you sincerely for putting me in Mind of introducing my Son to you. I will do so, when I am [in] Town. He will benefit of your Friendship, for he is in the Mercantile Business.

You are too polite a Man; for [you] pardon the Prolixity of my Letters. Indeed I should be still more impertinent in this way, only that my paper is a good Monitor, and–barely leaves me Room to assure you, that with my warmest affection to your whole Family, I am

Dr. Sir
Your most obliged and
Obed't. Serv't.
C. O'Conor

Charles O'Conor to George Faulkner
(Egerton 201, f-55)

Belanagare Sep. 25. 1767

Dear Sir

Last Monday I received your three Packetts of Lord Lyttleton's History (in Continuation) wherein your kind Letter of the 19th instant was enclosed. I thank you for both; and assuredly, I compute the Weight of obligation on my [self] by the Weight of Business which takes up your Time and which must stand still while you are thus ministring to my Improvement as well as Entertainment. You are satisfied with my Feelings, and are one of the few, who are so satisfied; and give their Friendship in return, for the Gratitude which themselves excite. What I rec'd. hitherto of Lord L's History concludes with Page 368, and leaves me in the midst of a very useful Digression on the Crusade War: a most extraordinary Suite of Events, wherein the Enthusiasm of *Some*; the Superstition of *others*, and the Ignorance of *all*, gave Rome a Dominion over Europe, superior to any it exerted in the Days of its Imperial Greatness! It was a Dominion over the human Mind and the most melancholy proof of Human Weakness. But Time broke the Charm: Mankind have acquired a little more Knowledge, and but a little, Since that Time; for we still evidently, wear some heavy Chains and[1] the few who shake them, or are shaking them off, bear no proportion to the many who are fond of them. I only wish that the Work of great Men like this you put into my hands, may open Men's Eyes. I request that you will give my Affections to *my Philosopher*, to Dr. Leland. I shall owe much to his Indulgence if he forgives me the Liberty I took with him in my Correspondence with you: It was a Liberty excited by my well-grounded Prejudices in his favor, and as you alone are privy to what I proposed to him, I can hardly repent of my Indiscretion, and especially, as you assure me that I am still in possession of his Friendship. I thank you warmly for Du Hamill's Agriculture.[2] Other books emprove and entertain [crossed out],[3] But such as Duhamil's qualify us for Emprovement, because thro' their help we establish our Independence the greatest of human Blessings. From [crossed out][4] the first of July to the 19th instant our weather was broken and very unpromising: for eight Days past we never had better. Our Hay and Corn are well saved and we have plenty of both. It is pleasing to see our people so busy in this provence. Men, Women, Children are grown industrious from the Introduction of the Linen Manufacture among us. Some of the Penal Laws which have put Restraints on the Industry of Papists, have been virtually repealed by the Course of Time, by the Necessity imposed by Nature, that Men can not thrive without each others Co-operation, and by the prevailing Genius of our Civil Constitution, which in spite of any By-Laws, permits [not] that Labor and Industry shall be quite unrewarded. I am encouraging the Linen Manufacture much in Belanagare, no Land in the County being more commodious for raising and watering Flax, and I am disposing of Matters so, as to render this Fragment of the Family Estate, much more valuable in a few years than it is at present. I have already subdued 200 Acres of coarse Land, and a District that never paid a Shilling to the Crown, pays now four pounds a year in Hearth Money. You have the Emprovement of your Native Country at heart, and if you had not, I would not be so ostentatious before you, relatively to the Emprovement of my part of it. To another this Account would be both vain and impertinent. Adieu my dear Sir, give my Affections to your Family and take Care of that Health in which your Friends, nay the public, are so much interested. I am assuredly

Sir,

your most obliged and obed. Serv't.

C. O'Conor

1. Approximately half a line is scratched out.
2. Faulkner advertised in his *Dublin Journal*, 14–18 July 1767, "In a few days will be published by George Faulkner, printer hereof, in two volumes octavo, *The Elements of Agriculture*, by M. Duhamel DuMonceau of the Royal Academy of Science in France and Fellow of the Royal Society in London." It would appear that Faulkner did not advertise this book for sale until September. It was Faulkner's usual practice to send prepublication copies to his friends. (See *Orrery Papers*, 2:23.) Whenever Faulkner suggested that the book "is soon to be published" rather than "in the press and soon to be published," he could be receiving the books unbound but already printed from London from the press of William Bowyer or Charles Reymer.
3. The section crossed out reads "the mind."
4. The word is crossed out, but reads "Since."

Charles O'Conor to George Faulkner
(Egerton 201, f–61)

Dear Sir

The personal Honours you have received from our Viceroy, both at Levee and at your own House, give me the strongest Impression of his Talents for Government. I am no way surprized, that a new Governor of Ireland, should seek an Acquaintanceship with its principal Citizens, particularly with you as he could not but have learned, that no Citizen in the Kingdom was better acquainted with its Men of Rank of all Professions and Principles. He must have heard, that they meet frequently under your Roof, and had (so to speak) long Sessions around your Table, where convivial enjoyments excluded all Reserve, except what Discretion and good Manners imposed. You know the proper Interests, you know the principal People of your Country, and you have *long known* both. And it is from such Men of Knowledge, who want and expect Nothing, that an able Minister will receive proper Information, stripped of all Disguises. There is hitherto no Agriculture Law, that properly is [manuscript deteriorated] could execute itself. The Wisdom of the Legislature would easily, I think, provide such a Law. Nothing on Earth could produce the Prosperity of this Island more effectively, and England evidently the great gainer by it. Such a Law would [gain] greater Glory to a great Minister, than a hundred Inscriptions, on the Pedestals of a hundred Marble Statues.

Our Popery Laws are so dispersed through our Statute Volumes, that the seeking them out in that detached Condition, is a very irksome Task. To draw them out under proper Heads and new Arrangement, would be a very useful Undertaking, and my Friend Councellor [Ridge][1] told me, that such a Disposition was made, and nearly executed. I shall enquire about this Matter as soon as I arrive in Town, and will give you all the Information I can get.

I request you will tender my Affections to Dr. Leland. He is not only a Man of great Learning, but what is infinitely better, a Man of great Knowledge. You surely made him very happy in the Company of that great Orientalist Mr. Scomberg. The Viceroy will gain Reputation by having such men in his Retinue. Great Ministers should know Books. Within their Pages, the Wisdom and Follies of Mankind, are best displayed; and the Knowledge is vastly of greater Importance to them, than to us, private Men.

The pamphlet describing the Lake of Kilarney and[2] admirable; and most poetically picturesque. I thank you greatly for the Pleasure I had in perusing[3] how Lord Lyttleton's first Volume of Henry II up to Page 400. Business and Entertainments abound upon you so much, at present, that I must suspend my own Gratification relatively to the Perusal of the Remainder of the Volume til I have the Pleasure thanking you in your own House. Meantime I send my Affections to your Family. I am most assuredly

Dear Sir,

Your most obliged and obedient Servant

Charles O'Conor

Belanagare. Nov. 24, 1767

1. John Ridge, Irish barrister, friend of O'Conor, Edmund Burke, and Oliver Goldsmith. For Goldsmith's comment on Ridge see Goldsmith's poem "Retaliation," in *Collected Works of Oliver Goldsmith*, ed. Arthur Friedman (Oxford: Clarendon Press, 1966), 4:153.
2. Manuscript corrupt.
3. Manuscript corrupt.

George Faulkner to Charles O'Conor
(*Royal Irish Academy, Dublin, B1.1, B1.2*[1])

Dublin, Nov. 7, 1766

Dear Sir

How can I possibly find Words to express my Gratitude to you for your many Favours to me, particularly for your last Letters. I read the first to Dr. Johnson, who is a real admirer of yours, and *was* much pleased with it. He returns you Thanks for the honourable Mention you have made of him in the Preface to your Dissertations and promised to write to you[2] [which I wish he may do, but he is grown so idle since he got his Pension, that he hath not wrote one Line from that to this date].[3] Dining with Lord Chesterfield at his Country Seat of Blackheath with the Earl and Countess of Blessington, Sir Thomas Robinson, our Primate's Brother,[4] and some others, they began to talk of Lord Taafe's Pamphlet (whom they never suspected to be an Author) and desired me to tell them what I knew of it. I told them I could give them no other Information than what your Letter contained, which gave them all very great Satisfaction, and they all said, I was very happy in so intelligent and good a Correspondent. Miss Smith is extreamly obliged to you for the kind Mention you have made of her, and presents her Thanks and Compliments to you. I could wish you were now in Dublin, that I might add to the Number of your learned and worthy Acquaintance, by introducing Mr. Howard of the Norfolk Family, whose Son is going to be marryed to Miss Copinger, Baron Mountney, etc.[5] who are delighted with your Charactor and Writings. Dr. Leland is much obliged to you for your honourable Mention of him. We never meet without toasting your Health. Mr. Bourke is gone to England to attend the Parliament. I wish I could have the Happiness of your dineing with me this Day, where you would meet Mr. Howard, his Son, Dr. Fitzsimons and my very good Friend, Mr. Anthony Dermot.[6]

Yesterday I had the Pleasure to dine with Judge Robinson, who told me that *The Candid Enquiry into the Causes and Motives of the Late Riots in the Province of Munster*, together with *A Brief Narrative of the Proceedings against these Rioters* was very true. [If you have not seen this Pamphlet I shall be glad to send it to you.][7] I was very happy in England having had the best Health and Spirits, with a large Acquisition of new Friends amongst the Learned, the Polite, the Agreeable and the Gracious. My Niece and I spent three very happy Days at Dr. Warner's in Surry, who has the highest Honour and Respect for you. His genteel Hospitality was more than Irish, as he gave my man William the Liberty of ranging throughout all the fruit Gardens, to feed on Peaches, Apricots, Nectarines, Plums, Melons, and Berries, etc. which all grew on Standards in the greatest Plenty. The Mulberry Trees were the largest I ever beheld, the Branches being linked together by great Bars of Iron, and planted above 200 Years. William eat [*sic*] no other Food the Time we were there, by which he was near losing his Life [by violent Lax].[8] Your Advice about my Health is extreamly kind and friendly. But what can I do who have such numerous Acquaintance? I will tell you, that I eat very little and slow; and never drink, but sip my Wine, as I do Tea, which prevents my Stomach from being clogged or over-loaded. I am very glad you have got rid of the Gout, with which Dr. Warner is tortured, [and at best, is obliged to be supported by great Poles. I am excessive glad of your Access to the College Library, as you will make an excellent use of it.][9] Judge Marshall, Dr. Delany, Dr. Leland, etc. present their best Respects and Compliments to you, and long much to see you in Dublin. [Our Privilege of Parliament being out, I shall not presume to apologize for the shortness of this Letter, as I should be most happy to pay the Weight in Gold and

even in brilliant Diamonds, from you and therefore][10] I most
humbly request that you will be pleased to write to me very
often, in which all my Family join, presenting their most
humble Respects to you with your very much obliged, most
humble and devout Servant

George Faulkner

1. The first two pages of this letter are bound in B1.1, the last line
of which reads, "my man William the Liberty of ranging throughout
all." The last page is bound with B1.2. The letter appears to be a
first draft, full of corrections and cross-outs. It was probably recopied
before it was sent to O'Conor.
2. See supra, O'Conor to Faulkner, 10 May 1757 and note.
3. Crossed out in the manuscript.
4. Sir Thomas Robinson (1700–1777) called "Long Sir Thomas."
His brother Richard was Bishop of Armagh, Lord Primate of Ireland.
5. In his *Dublin Journal*, 30 May–2 June 1767, Faulkner mentions
that "Charles Howard of Graystock, next Heir to his Grace, the Duke
of Norfolk set out from his home in Jermyn Street for Spa for recovery
of his Health." I would assume this is the same man that Faulkner
mentions in his letter.
6. Dr. Patrick Fitzsimons became Roman Catholic Archbishop of
Dublin in 1763. Anthony Dermott was a member of the Catholic
party.
7. See Gilbert, "Correspondence and Mss of Charles O'Conor,"
Appendix to the Eighth Report, 7:451, 484. The section which Faulkner crossed out in his first draft, "If you have not seen this Pamphlet
I shall be glad to send it to you," appeared in a revision of his letter
to O'Conor. O'Conor in a letter to Dr. John Curry on 2 December
1766 quoted the exact phrase. Unknown to Faulkner, O'Conor's friend
Curry had written the pamphlet. The English reviewer in the *Gentleman's Magazine* 38 (January 1767): 32, saw the pamphlet as "a mere
collection of different pieces, written with different views, and published in magazines in Ireland. The pretence of its being a letter to a
noble lord, is a stale trick to give it importance and excite curiosity."
8. Crossed out.   9. Crossed out.   10. Crossed out.

George Faulkner to Charles O'Conor[1]
(RIA, B1.2)

Dublin, Nov. 17, 1767

Dear Sir

Instead of my going to the Castle to wait on the Lord
Lieutenant, I was visited by his Excellency this Day Fort-

night, which was a very great Surprise upon me.[2] When he came to my Shop incognito attended by an Aid de camp, made Enquiry for me, asked was I at Home? Was I busy? Or any one with me? Upon which he was shewn into the Parlour when I was at Breakfast. He asked me how I did? Shook me by the Hand, when the Aid de camp whispered me, that that was the Lord Lieutenant; on which I desired his Excellency, to sit down, and then immediately entered into Conversation with me. Asked me the Reason I was not at the Castle? I said I was there twice. When? Once with the Lord Mayor, and once with the Merchants to address you. Then Sir, said he, Since you know the Way to the Castle, I shall be very glad to see you. On Friday following he called again to see me, looked at some Books, which he desired I would send Home. When I went to the Levee on Sunday the Aid de camps told me, I was enquired for by Lord Townsend, who directed, that I should be presented to him in the Drawing Room; which as soon as he entered, upon my being shewn to him, he came up to me, took me by the Hand, was very glad to see me there, and thanked me for my Expedition in sending him the Books, one Sett of which were Orrery's Pliny,[3] in which he wrote his Son's Name. All this happened in the Presence of Lords Spiritual and Temporal, the Speaker, the Judges, and many others of great Distinction. Previous to this I was visited by all his Household, excepting Lord Fredrick Campbell.[4]

If it be an Happiness I have that Pleasure of being visited by most Foreigners who come hither; and how can I help shewing them the Civilities of my Table, at which People of all Religions and Countries are very welcome. There are now two Gentlemen here in the Lord Lieutenant's Retinue, who are the most learned Gentlemen I ever met with, having travelled more and speaking greater Variety of Languages than I ever heard. Mr. Scomberg,[5] who dined with me last Thursday with Dr. Leland and some other Gentlemen, speaks and writes Arabic, Hebrew, all the Oriental Tongues equally with the English. There is a very clever Jew, one Jonas, come hither to show his Dexterity in Legerdemain. I never saw the fellow before. He is a very good Scholar, and speaks most European languages very well.[6] My Health still continues tolerably good and blessed be God, I am not afraid of Death, as I am very sure, *God will be merciful to me a Sinner, by the Death of our blessed Saviour.*

Can you inform me, where I can get the Penal Laws against the Roman Catholics of Ireland? It is for the first Man of this Kingdom. I believe my Friend, as you call him, is not the Author of the last Pamphlet against Lord Taafe's,[7] because I never heard him speak of it.

Well as Duhamill's Husbandry is wrote there is very little demand for it; but, when it is known, I doubt not, but the Sale may increase.

The present Bishop of Cloyne,[8] Brother to the Earl of Bristol, is a most agreeable, polite, well bred Man, and a great Enemy to Persecution, especially against the Catholicks of Ireland. Although you think of coming to Dublin very soon, yet I will not omit writing to you by this Post, as all my Letters inform me of heavy Rains and dreadful Innundations. You mention a Bill for the Security of Property in Books, and that I have Interest enough to get it enacted. I have not applyed for it, but Application hath been made to me by some leading Members for that Purpose, who have offered to bring it in, of which I have acquainted some Booksellers, who will consult upon it. As much hurryed as, indeed I am, I shall embrace every Opportunity of writing to you to convince you, that I am with greatest Gratitude, your much obliged, most obedient and humble Servant

George Faulkner

All my Family join with best respects to you.

1. Portions of this letter and the one n.d. 1768 appeared in Charles O'Connor's article "George Faulkner and the Irish Catholics," pp. 497–98. These letters appear in full for the first time.

2. Lecky, *A History of Ireland,* 2:109, states that Lord Townshend's period of administration as Lord Lieutenant (1767–1772) started out under benign circumstances. As Faulkner discovered, Townshend had an attractive personality which could win people to his side. He won other people to his point of view by bribes of peerages. Townshend spent the next five years trying to break the power of the Anglo-Irish gentry who had served as "undertakers." He prorogued Parliament for fourteen months until he could get a new election. He

packed both the Irish House of Commons and the House of Lords with his supporters. He controlled the Parliament until the House Ministry recalled him in 1772. Lecky, *A History of Ireland*, 2:116, repeated a commonplace which, no doubt, Faulkner heard said of the viceroy that "he was entirely destitute of tact and judgement, and he committed a fault which is peculiarly fatal in an Irish ruler. He sought for popularity by sacrificing the dignity and decorum of his position, and he brought both his person and his office into contempt."

3. Faulkner advertised in his *Dublin Journal*, 28 May–1 June 1751, that "Speedily will be publish'd by the Printer hereof in two volumes *The Letters of Pliny the Younger*, With Observations on each Letter; And an Essay on Pliny's Life addressed to Charles, Lord Boyle, by John Earl of Orrery." This book was one of the many which Faulkner periodically reoffered for sale with a new frontispiece printed for the occasion.

4. There is no positive identification here. It would appear that he is a son of the Duke of Argyle, whose titles include Earl of Campbell.

5. Ralph Schomberg (1714–1792), M.D., and antiquarian.

6. A word is crossed out here and is illegible.

7. O'Conor perhaps is referring to Henry Brooke, whose anti-Catholic *Letters from the Farmer to the Free and Independent Citizens of Dublin* Faulkner published in 1748–1749.

8. Frederick Augustus Hervey (1730–1803), Bishop of Cloyne (1767–1768). His brother, Augustus John Hervey, Earl of Bristol was Chief Secretary for Ireland (1766–1767).

George Faulkner to Charles O'Conor[1]
(RIA, B1.2)

Dear Sir

Friday last your Favour came to Hand, when I sent to Mr. Vesey to enquire about your Papers for Lord Lyttleton's History, but he was not in Town; but the next Day T. Todd saw him and shewed that part of your Letter about the Ms. you sent him, which he said he would send to his Lordship by that Post, and that he had wrote to you the Tuesday before. Soon after Todd returned from Mr. Vesey, Dr. Leland came to pay me a friendly Visit, as I have been confined for a Month past with the Gout in my only Foot and other Parts of me, and sometimes in my Hand, as you may see by this Writing, which was the Reason I did not write last Post.

Although the Privilege will expire next Saturday, pray write to me as often as you can, as your Letters give me the highest Pleasure. I have missed you very much since you left Dublin to have your Conversation in the most agreeable Companies. My Acquaintance daily multiplies by the Number of Strangers that visit me. I thank you for the Honour of my Lord Taaffe's calling to see me more than once before he left the Kingdom. He made me very happy by his polite Address and genteel Behaviour. He spoke most respectfully of you as every [one] must who has the Happiness of knowing you. My Lord Lieutenant continues to be extreamly civil to me. I have dined with him at Leaslip and at the Castle, and he hath done me the Honour to eat with me under my Roof, and the last Time Dr. Leland was of the Party. I never invite any of my Friends on these Occasions; but, request his Excellency to invite his own Friends, and to fill the Table, which he does with the best chosen People of Rank, Fortune, Learning, Wit, and Humour. I wish you were acquainted with his Excellency. You would be charmed with him for his Ease and Freedom. He likes Ireland better than any other Country in the World, particularly the Lake of Killarney, and all the hills of Cabrinkely near Dublin, and he says, that Quebec in America is the third Prospect in the World.[2] Todd and I are now drinking your Health in the finest garnet Color and the richest tasted Wine I ever saw. It is not Burgundy, Claret or Port. I know not what it is. It was a Present of a Gallon sent to me. I wish you were with us to share in the Delight of Sight, Smell and Flavour. You are tired, my hand is weak, and therefore, shall give you no further Trouble than to present the best Respects of all my Family, and subscribe myself your very much obliged and most humble Servant

George Faulkner

1. The date of this letter would appear to be sometime between 14 November 1768 and 10 January 1769. See Gilbert, "Correspondence and Mss of Charles O'Conor," *Appendix to the Eighth Report*, 7:491. O'Conor tells Dr. Curry of the same incidents in letters on these two dates.
2. Townshend commanded the British forces at Quebec after General Wolfe's death.

George Faulkner to Charles O'Conor
(RIA, B1.2)

Feb. 4, 1768

Dear Sir

I have read your Pamphlet with the greatest Pleasure and Instruction.[1] No Protestant could make more Objection to Catholicks than you have done, or do greater Honour to the Reign of King William. Bishop Traile must be very happy in your Opinion of his Sermon.[2] I told him my Sentiments upon it when I read the Ms. which now makes me very happy, as your Thoughts have coincided with mine. I wish to make all the World Friends and Agreeable to each other, and long to have a Day with you of Jews, Turks, Infidels, Hereticks, etc. with Christians and People of every Denomination, as I love to cure all Prejudices, and make the World happy, which is the sincere Design of your very much obliged, most obedient and humble Servant

George Faulkner

I shall publish as soon as you please.[3]

1. O'Conor's pamphlet was titled *A Vindication of Lord Taafe's Civil Principles in a Letter to the Author of a Pamphlet Entitled Lord Taafe's Observations upon the Affairs of Ireland Examined and Confuted.* See Gilbert, "Correspondence and Mss of Charles O'Conor," *Appendix to the Eighth Report,* 7:487.

2. Faulkner advertised for sale a sermon by Bishop Traile in the *Dublin Journal,* 12–15 December 1767, entitled *A Sermon Preached in Christ Church Dublin before the Rt. Hon. House of Lords on Thurs. the 5th of November 1767 being the Anniversary of the Gun Powder Treason and of the Landing of King William III,* by the Rt. Rev. Father in God, James, Lord Bishop of Down and Conor.

3. One wonders whether Faulkner's postscript to O'Conor was only a politeness or whether Faulkner deliberately advertised O'Conor's pamphlet early. The *Dublin Journal,* 30 January–2 February 1768, advertised that "This day is published . . . *A Vindication of Lord Taafe's Civil Principles.* . . ." Did some unforeseen difficulty delay Faulkner's selling the pamphlet until after O'Conor received Faulkner's letter of 4 February?

George Faulkner to Charles O'Conor
(RIA, B1.2)

Dublin, Jan. 16, 1772

Dear Sir

Inclosed I send you Lord Lyttleton's Letter to me, and shall obey his Commands in Regard to you.—I am now going on expeditiously with the two last Volumes of this Work, and am very sorry that Mr. Reily[1] is not in the Way to correct them, as he is very clever at that Business.

I hear that Dr. Leland's History is printing expeditiously in London; it will make three Volumes quarto, two of which I am told are sent over to him. What I tell is only heresay, as he has not yet mentioned that Affair to me, nor do I know who will reprint it here.

When you have read his Lordship's Letter (of which, if you please you may take a Copy) be so kind as to return it to me.

I could wish that you had wrote, and published your own History of Ireland, as no Person whatever is so well qualified as yourself.

Our Politics and Debates have run very high this Winter; which, with Mr. Howard's Epistles to me, and my notes thereon (one word of which neither of us wrote) have been great Entertainment to the Public, but Death to Mr. Howard, like the Boys and the Froggs; but, I laugh much at them—.[2]

When do you come to Town? I long much to see you. All my Family join in best Respects to you, and the Compliments of the Season with your very much obliged and most humble Servant

George Faulkner

1. There is no positive identification of Reily. E. R. Dix in Plomer's *Dictionary of Printers and Booksellers at Work in England, Scotland and Ireland, 1726–1775*, pp. 425–27, lists no Reily as printer or bookseller in Ireland at the time of this letter (1772). See "Correspondence and Mss of Charles O'Conor," *Appendix to the Eighth Report*, 7:458, 463, 478, 480, 481. This Reily would appear to be both copyreader, editor, and printer for the Catholic faction.

2. See the preface concerning the hoax Robert Jephson perpetrated

on Faulkner and Howard. Jephson's parody of Faulkner's rhetorical style in *An Epistle to Gorges Edmond Howard . . . by George Faulkner, Esq. and Alderman* kept Dublin laughing for months.

George Faulkner to Charles O'Conor
(RIA, B1.2)

Dublin, April 2, 1772

Dear Sir

The want of Franks prevented my answering your last Favour sooner.

I have seen Dr. Leland twice of late, whose History of Ireland is far advanced in the London Press; but, who will reprint it here I do not know: He takes much Pains with this Work, which greatly impairs his Health.

I often have heard of O'Flaherty's *Ogygia*[1] as being a Piece of great Merit and Truth; and very glad it is likely to be in your Hands, who will make it a Master Piece to which I should be Proud of the Honour of being the Printer and the publisher.

Lord Lyttleton hath made a very large Errata to his last Volume which I shall fix at the End.

I send the Remainder of the State of Denmark in different Covers by this Post.[2]

My family all join [with me][3] in best Respects to you with your very much obliged, most obedient humble Servant,

George Faulkner

1. See Gilbert, "Streets of Dublin," p. 37n. *Ogygia seu Rerum Hibernicarum Chronologia* was written by Roderic O'Flaherty (1629–1718), Irish historiographer who published his book in London in 1685 and used partial Gaelic type in its reproduction. O'Conor subsequently became editor of this reprint. Faulkner printed a subscription notice for this book in his *Dublin Journal*, 29 January–1 February 1774. He published the book ca. April 1775.

2. Faulkner advertised in his Dublin Journal, 18–20 February 1772, that he would soon have ready "in the press and will be speedily published" *The Present State of Denmark in Relation to Its Govern-*

113

ment, Trade and Manufacturers, Its Revenue and Forces. . . . In a Series of Letters mostly written by Monsieur Roger.
3. Crossed out.

George Faulkner to Charles O'Conor
(RIA, B1.2)

Dublin, April 28, 1772

Dear Sir

Moran's[1] other Letter being published, I inclose it to you –Did you ever meet with Laurence's Interest of Ireland?[2] I am now reading it, and think he is very partial and credulous. This Book was printed 90 years ago (1682) since which time I do not think our Country much improved, although we have had 80 years Peace.

This Day I had a Visit from our Friend Dr. Leland who is quite recovered, and sends Compliments to you, as do Mr. Todd and all my family with your very much obliged,

most obedient and humble Servant
George Faulkner

1. Unidentifiable.
2. *British Museum General Catalogue of Printed Books,* 132:15, identifies this author and book as Richard Lawrence, *The Interest of Ireland in Its Trade and Wealth Stated* (London, 1692).

George Faulkner to Charles O'Conor
(RIA, B1.2)

Dublin, Sept. 3, 1772

Dear Sir

The inclosed Letter from Lord Lyttleton is in Answer to the one I lately wrote to him. When you have read it, I request you will be pleased to send it to me.

I am extreamly concerned that Mr. M'Dermott your Son-in-Law did not favour me with more of his Company; and I am very angry that he did not introduce me to his Son, as he promised; when he comes next to Dublin, I shall request that Favour. I have been told that Lord Lyttleton is correcting and preparing for the Press a Collection of all his Works; I am also told, that Dr. Johnson is also augmenting his Dictionary for a new Edition in Folio. I should be very glad that you would do so for your Dissertation. What have you done about O'Flaherty's Oygygia, and the French Abbe's History of Ireland? I made Major Vallency[1] very happy yesterday by sending him the enclosed Letter; and he intended to write to his Lordship on the Subject, and return him Thanks for the honourable Mention he has made of him. Did the Major send you the Information upon St. Patrick's Tomb at Armagh? No one here can read or construe it. I hope you can, and will send me the Interpretation thereof.

I hear that Lord Harcourt is expected here the middle of next Month, that he has appointed one Mr. Jones for his first Chaplain; Major Buxton and three other Gentlemen of Lord Townshend's Aid de camp to be his; Mr. Swan[2] Controller. . . .[3]

1. Major Charles Vallency (1721–1812), retired engineer officer and antiquarian. He edited a collection of Irish pieces called *Collectanea de Rebus Hibernicus* (1770–1805).
2. Jones, Buxton, and Swan are not otherwise identified.
3. The rest of the letter is missing.

George Faulkner to Charles O'Conor
(RIA, B1.2)

Dublin, Nov. 11, 1773

Dear Sir
Being very much confined with Gout, Asthma and Cramps, I do not often go abroad, although I have a Carriage, in which I should be proud of having often Times the

Pleasure of your most agreeable and improving Conversation.

Lord Lyttleton's Death[1] is a great Loss to the Public, but particularly to me, as he always treated me with the greatest Civility and Politeness, and I may add with sincere Friendship. I am very sorry I did not see him some Time before his Death, as a Gentleman who was in great intimacy, who lately come to Ireland, told me that his Lordship wanted very much to see me, and to spend some Days at his delightful Seat at Hagley's.

Whatever his Lordship said to you by Letters or otherwise, your own great Merit justly entitled you thereto.

The Society of Antiquarians, by electing you an honorary Member, did themselves great Credit, in having so learned and respectable a Gentleman among them as you are.

I saw Major Vallency at the Dublin Society last Thursday, who told me that he got your Tract[2] and would send it to Dr. Leland, and write to you. Dr. Leland has been most happy and much benefited by your Acquaintance in the History of Ireland, as well as in other Affairs.

Dr. Warner's eldest or, I believe only Son,[3] was lately in this Kingdom. He is most agreeable and conversible, having not only made the Grand Tour, but travelled through Germany, Spain, Portugal and other Countries, of which he gives the most Accurate and pleasing Accounts. He hath seen most Parts of England, and came through Scotland hither, landed at Donaghadee,[4] saw the principal Towns in the North, says the Church at Hillsborough far surpasses any other Church that he hath seen on the Continent, that is not a Cathedral; it is built in the Gothic Style, 150 ft. in Length and above 60 broad, has a fine Ring of eight Bells, and a very grand Organ. The whole is at Lord Hillsborough's Expense, above 17,000 £. He was also at Armagh, where the Primate[5] is doing Wonders in repairing and adding ornamental Structures to the old Cathedral; has built a very grand Palace, a large Market House, Library, Infirmary, Alms Houses, etc. and all at his own Expense. He is also building Churches in his Diocese, to which he gives 20,000 £ out of his own Pocket. Young Dr. Warner I should have told you was at that wonderful place, The Gyant's Causeway, which more than answered all he read or talked of. Upon his Arrival at Dublin, some other Friends and I shewed him the Environs of Dublin, with which he was ravished. After this he went to the Lake of Killarney, which surpasses all the natural Beauties he ever beheld, and which no Words or Painting can describe. After this Journey he went to the County of Wicklow, where he says, the Prospects far surpass those of Mount Edgeumbe, which are allowed to be the most beautiful in England. I could have wished that you were in Dublin when he was here, as he would have pleased you. He says, upon the Whole, there is not so fine a Country, or so good a Climate in Europe, as Ireland is.

November 16. On Account of very bad Health, I could proceed no further than the foregoing–I am very glad that O'Flaherty's Oygygia has been approved of by the Committee of Antiquarians. No Person whatever can be so proper to publish that Work as yourself.–Should I be so happy as to publish it, I shall not stop at any Expense in paying for it, although from my Age and Infirmities, I am getting out of the Bookselling Business; and, if you print it on your own Account, by Subscription, I will endeavour to do you every Service, which you are justly entitled to.

I hear, and sincerely wish it may be true, that Bills are to be brought into Parliament to empower Bishops to let Leases of their Lands for 61 Years, and that Roman Catholics will have the same Tenures, or three Lives.[6]

I am extreamly sorry for the Migrations from your almost depopulated Country, which must end in the inevitable Ruin of Ireland, as most human Beings are flying from it.[7]

Can there be any thing more surprizing than our (pretended) Patriots[8] opposing the Tax upon Irish Absentees? The Americans, and all other Nations, who have a Sense of Liberty and Property, loudly complain of such Grievances, and must Ireland be the only Country of Slavery and Oppression? I send you an American Pamphlet on this melancholy Subject, which ought to be read by every Hibernian. Your Letters to me are always too short, and mine are too tedious, for which, I hope you have good Nature and Patience to excuse your very much obliged, most obedient, humble Servant

George Faulkner

Mr. Todd and all my Family send best Respects to you and yours.

1. 22 August 1773 at Hagley, Worcestershire.
2. See *Dictionary of National Biography*, 14:856, *A Statistical Account of the Parish of Kilroman*.
3. John Warner (1736-1800), classical scholar and divine.
4. John Warner landed at Donaghadee on the northeast peninsula of County Down. In order to go to the Giant's Causeway, northwest of Donaghadee, he could go due east to Belfast, north to Ballymena and Ballycastle, and west along the coast to the Giant's Causeway. Moving south he would go through Port Stewart, Coleraine, south to Derry, Strabane, and Omagh, east and south to Dungannon and Armagh, south and east to the coast to Dundalk, Drogheda, and finally, Dublin.
5. Richard Robinson, Archbishop of Armagh and later created Baron Rokeby of Armagh in 1777.
6. Lecky, *A History of Ireland*, 2:193, noted that in 1774 a bill "for enabling Catholics under certain conditions to take leases for lives was introduced in the House of Commons, but it appears it was not carried beyond its earliest stages."
7. Lecky, *A History of Ireland*, 1:247, estimates that over 4,000 emigrants sailed from Belfast to the continent and America.
8. See Lecky, *A History of Ireland*, 2:125, for comment on Edmund Burke on the Absentee Tax. Burke was one of these "pretended patriots."

George Faulkner to Charles O'Conor
(*RIA, B1.2*)

Dublin, Dec. 11, 1773

Dear Sir

Could you imagine that I should ever neglect answering any Letter from you? I have always Pleasure in receiving your Epistles, and in the reading of them. In the Letter I sent a Month or five Weeks ago, I told you, that I had seen Major Valency who got your Ms.—I since met Dr. Leland at the

Dublin Society, who told me he got it, but not the Ogygia. A Gentleman, to my very great Concern brought me a Message that I had not answered your Last, which, I assured him I had, and called upon the Servant whom I sent to the Post Office, who offered to make Oath before the Priest, then sitting with me, that he put the two Letters into the Post Office for you. What can I do? If he has deceived me, I will discharge him for being a lying Scoundrel. At the same Time that I wrote to you I sent a Pamphlet under two covers upon American Affairs, and desired your Opinion of it.[1] The Writer is said to be the ingenious Dr. Franklin, an American by Birth and a Quaker. Your Dissertations are out of Print. Any Work that you undertake by Subscription I shall give all the Aid and Assistance in my Power thereto. Your Notes and Comments on Ogygia, will make a most valuable Work. I mentioned when I last wrote to you, that I had a Carriage, and should think myself extreamly happy in being honoured with your most agreeable and entertaining Company–My health is but indifferent, although, I had a most agreeable and pleasing Lodging in the Country last Summer at Knockmaroon Hill, near Chapel-Izod, which afforded very pleasing Prospects and good Air. Had the Gentlemen you sent to me about your Letter and the Miscarriage of my Answer to it, that you would have been in Town that Night or the Day following, I should have wrote to you by the next Post, but, not seeing or hearing from him since, I now write this to you to justify myself, and to assure you that I am, with all the Compliments of my Family, your very much obliged

Most obedient humble Servant,

George Faulkner

1. Possibly Benjamin Franklin's "Rules for Reducing a Great Empire to a Small One." See "Q.E.D.", "Rules for Reducing a Great Empire to a Small One," *Gentleman's Magazine* 43 (September 1773): 441 ff.

George Faulkner to Charles O'Conor
(RIA, B1.2)

Dear Sir

I have had the Pleasure of knowing, and of being Acquainted with Dean Woodward[1] for several Years past, and have always found him a Gentleman of exceeding good Character, an excellent Pastor, and most useful to the Public. By his Foundation of the House of Industry he hath banished at least nine Beggars in ten from the Streets of Dublin, which will every Day be more healthful as they are pulling down the Signs, Posts, Rails, and Pest Houses.

I have got your Notes for seven Sheets of Ogygia, which, I hope, and make no Doubt, will answer with you, although the List of Subscribers do not at present, many People objecting to pay before hand, being often disappointed by the Works never being printed, and many will buy yours when finished.

I shall be glad, of your Opinion of young Lord Lyttleton's Speech against Earl Chatham.[2] I know his Lordship very well, as he did me the Honour to call frequently to see, and dined with me when he was in Dublin: He is a young Nobleman of great Abilities, who, I'm sure would act consistently with himself; but there is no Perfection in human Beings. I am with best Respects to you and Family, in whom Mrs. Rogers[3] and Mr. Todd join with your much obliged and humble Servant

George Faulkner

Dublin, July 18, 1774

1. See Constantia Maxwell, *Dublin under the Georges* (London: Faber and Faber, 1956), p. 157. Richard Woodward (1726–1794), D.D.; his pamphlet *An Argument in Support of the Right of the Poor in Ireland to a National Provision* helped to gain support for a public workhouse in Dublin.
2. Faulkner published the substance of Lyttleton's reply to Lord Chatham's speech on the Quebec bill in the *Dublin Journal*, 30 June–2 July 1774.
3. There is no positive identification of Mrs. Rogers. Perhaps she was Faulkner's housekeeper.

Memoranda from George Faulkner

(Egerton 201, f-6)

Sunday April 3, 1774[1]

I George Faulkner was 71 years old and entered into my 72nd for which I return my most humble and grateful Thanks to my great Creator Supporter, and Benefactor, God Almighty and Jesus Christ my [Saviour crossed out] Saver and Redeemer.

1. This memorandum would place George Faulkner's birth in 1702. Most writers place his birth in 1699. If he were born in 1702 he would have been of the right age to apprentice with Thomas Hume in 1716. However, the transcript of his gravestone records his age as seventy-six when he died in 1775. There is no way one can tell which date is wrong.

August 19, 1774

This Day Earl Harcourt, Lord Lieutenant of Ireland, Lord Sifford, L. High Chancellor, Earl of Westmeath, Hon. Thomas Fitzmaurice,[1] Colonel Skeen,[2] Mr. Wallis,[3] Alderman French, W. Lees,[4] Captain Jephson,[5] W. Butler,[6] Captain Loftus,[7] and Captain Schomberg,[8] Tho. Todd and Faulkner dined in Parliament Street with G. Faulkner, and all were most agreeable.

1. Thomas Fitzmaurice would seem to be a relative of Lord Kerry.
2. Unidentified.
3. Unidentified.
4. Unidentified.
5. Robert Jephson, Master of Horse to three Lord Lieutenants, Halifax, Townshend, and Harcourt.
6. Unidentified.
7. Unidentified.
8. Captain Alexander Schomberg, commander of the Lord Lieutenant's yacht.

Eulogy for George Faulkner

It is with peculiar Satisfaction the Author of this little Piece can draw a Character of a Man without being suspected of interested Views or the Truth of his Colouring called in Question; for few Authors choose to flatter the Dead but pay their Court to the Living; A few Bards are so impolite as not to hail the rising Sun—George Faulkner was an Honour to his Profession, nay, the Ornament of Humanity. At his Table [decent] Wit and chastised Mirth took their Place. His Guests were the Friends of Literature, the great Officers of the State, and the Fathers of the City. He disdained not to take Merit by the Hand in whatever shabby Vestments it was cloathed; nay, he would seek for it in its Shade of Obscurity and draw it into Day. But if his Affability, his Condescension, his Hospitality were great, his Interest and Public Spirit were still greater. Unabashed by Favour, unmoved by Solicitations, he still preserved an Independence that still let him to follow the Dictates of an honest Heart. Distress never lived for him in Vain; nor did he send the Solicitors for charitable Subscriptions empty away. His Love of his Country was so great that nothing could ever induce him to betray her Interests, or to promote Measures he imagined prejudicial to her. Those who differed from him in their political Sentiments, honoured his Integrity; and though they might think the Politician sometimes wrong they acknowledged the *Man* was ever in the right. To be brief George Faulkner exhibited a faithful Picture of the "Noblest Work of God" possessing an admirable Integrity, an amiable Personality, the purest Patriotism; and for unbounded Hospitality he ever displayed to Men of all Parties, well deserved the affectionate Apellation given him by his noble Friend, the late Lord Chesterfield, the Hibernian Atticus.

ANON.

(BM Egerton 201, f-8)

125

Notes

1. *Dublin Journal*, 29 October–3 November 1745. *Irish Newspapers in Dublin Libraries before 1750.*
2. *Dublin Journal*, 17–20 April 1742.
3. *Dublin Journal*, 11–15 January 1742/43.
4. 18–20 March 1746/47.
5. *Dublin Journal*, 22–26 December 1747.
6. 17–20 July 1731.
7. *Dublin Journal*, 5–8 September 1741.
8. *Dublin Journal*, 10–13 February 1753, *The Dublin Journal and the Freeman's Journal, 1750–1825*, vol. 2.
9. 19–23 January 1762.
10. *Dublin Journal*, 19–23 January 1762.
11. Jonathan Swift, *The Correspondence of Jonathan Swift*, 4:222 (hereafter cited as *Correspondence*).
12. Anonymous, "Authentic Memoirs of the Late George Faulkner, Esq.," p. 503; see also "Viscount Dillon," in *Burke's Genealogical and Heraldic History of the Peerage, Baronetage, and Knightage*, p. 816. Faulkner's obituary writer maintains that Faulkner's mother was related to the noble Dillon family; however, her father did not receive any land in the 1660 land court hearings. Also members of the Dillon family under Viscount Dillon left Ireland with the Irish brigades for service with the French. An ancestor, Catholic and Jacobite, such as Viscount Dillon might help to explain Faulkner's relaxed attitudes with such Catholic notables as Charles O'Conor and Archbishop Fitzsimmons.
13. "Authentic Memoirs," p. 504.
14. See James L. Clifford, *Young Samuel Johnson*, pp. 47, 52, 58. Faulkner's education must have included the traditional classical education similar to Samuel Johnson's from age seven to fourteen. He probably used Lily's *Grammar* and after his tenth year proceeded to read Cicero and some of Ovid and Cato.
15. H. R. Plomer, *Dictionary of Printers and Booksellers at Work in England, Scotland and Ireland, 1668–1725*, p. 503, finds that Thomas Hume was at work in Copper Alley near Essex Street from 1715 to 1728. If Faulkner were apprenticed at the age of fourteen, then he must have served another printer, not Hume, before 1715. However, if we accept his statement (supra, April 1774) that he was born in 1702 then he could have entered his apprenticeship with Hume in 1716.
16. John Nichols, *Literary Anecdotes of the Eighteenth Century*, 3:208. Faulkner's letter to Nichols mistakenly mentions 1726

as the year when Faulkner worked for William Bowyer, Sr. K. I. T. Maslen, senior lecturer in English at the University of Otago, Dunedin, New Zealand, called my attention to the original holograph letter in the Cambridge University Library. Faulkner was in some doubt as to the year, since he crossed out what appeared to be either "1721" or "1727" in the original letter and inserted "1726" which Nichols printed in his *Literary Anecdotes*. If Faulkner were working for Bowyer in 1721, he would have met young Bowyer when he returned from Cambridge in 1722.

17. Presumably Faulkner returned to Dublin from London in 1724. *The Catalogue of the Bradshaw Collection of Irish Books at the University Library, Cambridge*, 1:173, records a book for 1724 without a Faulkner imprint but with ornaments identical to other signed Faulkner works in the collection.

18. Faulkner's *Dublin Post-Boy*, 21 January 1725/26. "Printed by George Faulkner in Pembroke Court, Castle-street." The first issue I have seen is number eight. Counting back to the original issue, one assumes Faulkner started the *Post-Boy* either December 25 or 26. Faulkner printed the *Post-Boy* on Mondays and Fridays and the *Journal* on Tuesdays and Thursdays; Jonathan Swift, *Prose Works of Jonathan Swift*, 3:201 (hereafter cited as *Prose Works*).

19. "Authentic Memoirs," p. 504. Faulkner's biographer asserts that Faulkner married a Widow Taylor during his first trip to England. One assumes that this marriage took place sometime before 22 October 1726. His *Journal* for 25-29 October 1726 included a note to his customers mentioning his absence from London. *Prose Works*, 13:201, leaves the impression that Faulkner was prosperous if he were going to London one year after opening his shop.

20. *Dublin Journal*, 23-27 August 1726.

21. *Dublin Journal*, 18-21 November 1727, "Printed by George Faulkner and James Hoey in Christ Church Yard"; Robert Munter, *The History of the Irish Newspaper, 1685-1760*, p. 25.

22. *Prose Works*, 12:336; *Dublin Journal*, 21-24, 25-28 March 1730. Faulkner prints the following in his edition for 21-24 March, "Shops in Essex Street and Skinner's Row." Faulkner never gave any reason for his break with James Hoey. Perhaps Hoey's bitterness stemmed from his jealousy brought on by Jonathan Swift's preference for Faulkner's company.

23. *Dublin Journal*, 5-8 September 1730: "On Wednesday the 2nd Inst. George Faulkner, Printer in Essex-street, embark'd on the Racehorse for England: the said Faulkner did some time since print an ingenious and witty Pamphlet, entitled *Graffanio-Mastix, or a Collection of Poems on the Censor*: Some People will have it, that the said Pamphlet reflects heavily on a certain learned Body, who, upon those supercilious Grounds, have, it seems order'd a Prosecution against said Faulkner, to shun which, his Enemies give out, he is fled to England. I therefore beg leave to assure the World, that I am not under the least Apprehension of Danger from said Prosecution (being oblig'd to absent myself at this Time, Matters of Moment demanding my Attendance in England) and that I design to be ready against Term, to answer unto whatever may be alleg'd against Me, if my Affairs will conveniently permit." / September 2, 1730. / George Faulkner.

24. *Dublin Journal*, 12-15 June 1731.
25. "Authentic Memoirs," pp. 504 ff.
26. H. R. Plomer et al., *Dictionary of Printers and Booksellers at Work in England, Scotland and Ireland, 1726-1775*, pp. 425 ff.
27. Richard Robert Madden, *The History of Irish Periodical Literature from the End of the Seventeenth Century to the Middle of the Nineteenth Century*, 2:10.
28. *Dublin Journal*, 7-11 January 1728/29.
29. Munter, *The History of the Irish Newspaper, 1685-1760*, p. 65.
30. John T. Gilbert, *History of the City of Dublin* (London, 1854), 2:32.
31. *The Orrery Papers*, ed. Emily DeBurgh Canning, Countess of Cork and Orrery (London, 1903), 2:23.
32. "Authentic Memoirs," p. 571.
33. Louis A. Landa, *Swift and the Church of Ireland*, pp. 114 ff.; *Prose Works*, 13:204.
34. William Blackstone, *Of Public Wrongs*, 2:158.
35. *Prose Works*, 13:204.
36. *Prose Works*, 13:205.
37. *Correspondence*, 5:256n, 257.
38. 6-10 February 1732/33.
39. *Correspondence*, 4:166.
40. *Correspondence*, 4:222. One can only conjecture what Swift's motives were. Perhaps he felt that this edition by an Irish printer would be a grave joke on the English.
41. *Correspondence*, 4:231.
42. Hastings Mss, Part 3, vol. 77 (London: Historical Manuscripts Commission, 1934), p. 19.
43. *Dublin Journal*, 6-10 February 1732/33; 5-9 November 1734; 23-26 November 1734; Herman Teerink, *Bibliography of the Writings of Jonathan Swift*, p. 26.
44. *Dublin Journal*, 7-11 January 1734/35.
45. *Dublin Journal*, 25 February-1 March 1734/35.
46. *Dublin Journal*, 1-4 February 1734/35.
47. "Authentic Memoirs," pp. 505, 571.
48. "Authentic Memoirs," p. 505.
49. *Correspondence*, 4:482.
50. A. S. Collins, *Authorship in the Days of Samuel Johnson*, pp. 60, 74 ff.; Donald Cornu, "Swift, Motte, and the Copyright Struggle: Two Unnoticed Documents," pp. 118 ff.
51. *Correspondence*, 4:493.
52. *Correspondence*, 5:21.
53. Reginald H. Griffith, *Alexander Pope: A Bibliography, 1735-1751*, vol. 1, pt. 2, p. 426; *Dublin Journal*, 17-20 June 1741; *The Correspondence of Alexander Pope*, 1:xv; 4:270-98, 314, 320-23, 330-32, 333n. The following is a chronological chart of the whereabouts of the "clandestine volume," 1740-1741:

May 1740   Printed by Pope and given to Samuel Gerrard, who delivered it to Jonathan Swift in Dublin.

July   By 29 July Faulkner is printing from "clan-

	destine volume" which he received from Swift.
August	Pope writes Faulkner a letter demanding that he (Faulkner) stop printing the letter for 13 August (the letter is not extant). Faulkner does not receive the letter until September and subsequently stops printing from the "volume."
September	Faulkner accedes to Pope's request and takes the volume and sheets to show Lord Orrery.
4 October	Pope writes Faulkner and asks to see the volume and what Faulkner has printed.
18 October	Orrery sends the printed volume to Faulkner in four packages.
8 November	Orrery asks for return of the volume and the sheets on the pretext of looking at it. Orrery has written Pope that he (Orrery) will pretend to keep them and, unknown to Faulkner, send them to Pope in London for corrections.
15 November	Orrery receives volume and sheets from Faulkner and sends them to Pope.
10 December	Pope receives the packet.
27 December	Pope returns volume to Orrery except pages 1–23 which he keeps.
12 January 1740/41	Orrery receives the packet. In a letter of the same date to Pope, Orrery suggested, "The best method we can pursue will be to give him (Faulkner) back the letters." Probably Orrery did this before sailing to England in February. On 29 January 1741, Pope wrote to Orrery, "When you are at Dublin ingage Falkener to send hither a book the moment he publishes; and to return the foul copy by which he prints." The foul copy according to Professor Sherburn was the "clandestine volume." Pope wanted it to prevent Faulkner's recognizing its similarity to Pope's London edition when that edition appeared. Presumably Pope destroyed the "clandestine volume" after he had achieved his purpose.

54. *Dublin Journal*, 22–25 January 1742/43. "The Printer hereof having got two hundred Subscribers for that great and useful Work *The Universal History from the Earliest Account of Time to the Present: Compiled from the Original Authors and Illustrated with Maps, Cuts, Notes Chronological and other Tables* in eight volumes Folio, takes this Opportunity of returning his Thanks to those Noblemen, Ladies, and Gentlemen, who have been pleased to countenance this Work, and is much obliged to them who have already paid their first

subscription of 4 Guineas each and declares and desires their Favour of such as have given their Name, that they will be pleased to pay the above Sum that the Work may be put to Press by 25th March next out of regard to them without a View to any further Subscription which will then be closed; after which Time the Price will be raised to twelve pounds according to the Proposals." Faulkner modified this edition to seven volumes, folio.

55. *Dublin Journal*, 18–22 September 1744. "We the undersigned Booksellers being sensible how destructive such Attempts are to so unstable a Branch of Business as the printing Trade in this Kingdom, are resolved at any Expense to put a Stop to such Practices for the Future. We therefore have determined in conjunction with Mr. Faulkner, to reprint said Work in twenty Volumes, Octavo.... Next Week will be published Proposals with Specimens annex'd to be had at the following Bookseller's Shops, viz. George Faulkner, R. Gunne, R. Owen, G. Risk, G. and A. Ewing, W. Smith, P. Crampton, A. Bradley, T. Moore, E. Exshaw, W. Powell, T. Butler, J. Hoey, and O. Nelson, W. Brien, T. Butler." This edition, completed in twenty volumes, octavo, Faulkner advertised for sale on 20 May 1746; *Dublin Journal*, 11–14 May 1745. Faulkner advertised the near completion of his folio edition when he commented that the "seventh and last volume" was "in the press." Faulkner is in error here. I have seen the eight-volume folio edition at the National Library of Ireland, Dublin.

56. *Dublin Journal*, 5–9 June 1744.

57. *Dublin Journal*, 19–22 October 1745.

58. Dr. Mathew Maty's four volume edition of *The Miscellaneous Works of the Late Philip Dormer Stanhope, Earl of Chesterfield* is the earliest edition I have seen of Chesterfield's letters. Possibly it was the first to incorporate the Faulkner letters in the edition. Maty's volume 4 is entitled *Letters to S. Dayrolles and Other Friends*. Later editions by Lord Mahon, John Bradshaw, depend on this. Bonamy Dobree used the Chesterfield letters from British Museum, Egerton 201 collection.

59. Maty, *Miscellaneous Works*, 4:86. I used this early edition because all letters of Chesterfield to Faulkner that are used by later editors are in this one edition.

60. Maty, *Miscellaneous Works*, 4:81.

61. For Orrery's statement to Thomas Carew see *Orrery Papers*, 2:23; Gilbert, *History of the City of Dublin*, 2:34 ff.

62. Mrs. Mary Delany, *The Autobiography and Correspondence of Mary Granville, Mrs. Delany*, 3:79.

63. *Correspondence*, 4:493; Jonathan Swift, *The Correspondence of Dr. Jonathan Swift, D.D.*, ed. F. Elrington Ball (London, 1913), 6:223 ff.

64. *Dublin Journal*, 10–14 February 1740/41; Allan McKillop, *Samuel Richardson*, missed this advertisement: "This day is published by George Faulkner and George Ewing, *Pamela or Virtue Rewarded*. In a Series of familiar Letters from a beautiful young Damsel to her Parents. ... As the Demand for this Book is expected to be very great, it is hoped that Gentlemen will be pleased to send Silver, since it is very difficult to provide change." Richardson, the printer-novelist, was a business acquaintance of Faulkner. Richardson's importance as

printer and bookseller has been noted by McKillop; however, William Sale, Jr., in *Samuel Richardson: Master Printer* (Ithaca, N.Y.: Cornell University Press, 1950), indicates the extent of Richardson's importance in London. He shows that Richardson was a member of the Stationer's Guild as early as 1727 (p. 30). Moreover, his abilities and, perhaps more important, his influence gained him lucrative printing contracts for the House of Commons. In 1733 he began printing bills for the House (p. 77) and from 1741 to 1754 he helped print the journals of the House of Commons (p. 80).

65. McKillop states (p. 87) that since the novel was so much in demand, "George Faulkner and George Ewing got out an unauthorized edition of *Pamela* early in 1741." He footnotes the charge as follows: "Faulkner's *Dublin Journal* March 17–21, 1741 advertises a reprint called the 'second edition'." One assumes that he designates the term "second edition" as his proof that this is a pirated edition. Is it not more probable that the second edition refers to the Faulkner edition of 10–14 February rather than the London edition? Samuel Richardson's hysterical "Address to the Public," bound at the end of his *Sir Charles Grandison*, 3d ed., twelvemo (London, 1754), 7:424–42, has done much to prejudice future literary historians in believing that George Faulkner was a thieving rascal. Compare for negative opinions of Faulkner: Anna Laetitia Barbauld, "The Life of Mr. Richardson," *The Correspondence of Samuel Richardson* (London, 1804), 1:cxlv, 6 ff.; Clara L. Thompson, *Samuel Richardson* (London, 1900), p. 54; Austen Dobson, *Samuel Richardson* (London, 1901), pp. 165 ff.; Brian Downs, *Samuel Richardson* (London, 1928), pp. 25 ff.; Paul Dottin, *Samuel Richardson: Imprimeur des Londres* (Paris, 1931), pp. 168, 258–60, 389 ff.; and McKillop, *Samuel Richardson*.

66. Richardson, *Grandison*, 7:429n.

67. Richardson, *Grandison*, 7:426.

68. Samuel Johnson, *Letters of Samuel Johnson*, 1:55. "My Lord Corke is desirous to see Mr. Falkner's letter to me, I wish you would send it him as by my desire, and when it is returned, take care to keep it for my justification, for I would not have shewn it, but at his own instigation." The letter is not extant.

69. Richardson, *Grandison*, 7:440. "If this is the case, and nothing can be more probable (for Wilson hath, by affidavitt before the Lord Mayor, purged himself of the corruption and Exshaw and Saunders declare they can do the same), then Mr. ******** [asterisks match letters of Faulkner's name] is still more evidently the scandalous Associate of the Corruptors, inasmuch as he conceals the most criminal, and, in some measure, abets the rest." Richardson, *Grandison*, 7:438; Chapman, *Letters of Samuel Johnson*, 1:55n. The person whom Richardson mentions in asterisks when he chides Faulkner for writing to him, matches the number of letters in Samuel Johnson's surname.

70. Nichols, *Literary Anecdotes of the Eighteenth Century*, 4:592.

71. Gilbert, *History of the City of Dublin*, 2:38.

72. Brian Fitzgerald, "The Earl of Kildare and Archbishop Stone," pp. 40 ff.; William Edward Hartpole Lecky, *A History of Ireland in the Eighteenth Century*, 1:464 ff.

73. *Dublin Journal*, 29 January–2 February 1754.

74. *Dublin Journal*, 12–16 February 1754.

75. Gilbert, *History of the City of Dublin*, 2:37.

76. *Orrery Papers*, 2:121, reads "honour," whereas the holograph copy from Dr. Barry to Lord Orrery, *Orrery Papers*, "A Series of Letters from Ireland," Mss English 218.5 Houghton Library, Harvard University, Cambridge, Mass., p. 73, reads in the last line "dishonour."

77. *Orrery Papers*, 2:120.

78. Maty, *Miscellaneous Works*, 3:360.

79. *Dublin Journal* Extraordinary, 21 February 1754.

80. *Dublin Journal*, 7-11 January 1755. Faulkner says, "If there be any Mistakes or Omissions in this Day's Journal, it is hoped that the Publick will excuse them on account of the Death of Mrs. Faulkner, Wife of the Printer hereof, who died Yesterday Morning a most painful and lingering Illness which she bore with the most Christian Patience and Resignation. By her Death her Acquaintance have lost a most agreeable and sincere Friend, and the Poor, especially reduced Housekeepers a most liberal and charitable Benefactress."

81. Charles O'Connor, "George Faulkner and the Irish Catholics," p. 497; 28 December-1 January 1736/37 Faulkner begins printing agricultural experiments recommended by the Dublin Society. Faulkner printed weekly observations from members of the Dublin Society for such varied projects as raising and dressing flax (Jan. 1), raising hops in red bog (May 17), and road building (May 24).

82. Maty, *Miscellaneous Works*, 3:269.

83. Mathew O'Conor, *History of the Irish Catholics from the Settlement in 1691, With a View of the State of Ireland from the Invasion of Henry II to the Revolution*, p. 254; Charles O'Connor, "George Faulkner and the Irish Catholics," p. 493; letters supra, O'Conor to Faulkner, 10 May, 25 May 1757.

84. See letters supra, Faulkner to Derrick, 4 October 1760 and 14 May 1761.

85. 3 6 October 1761.

86. *Dublin Journal*, 3-6 October 1761.

87. *Dublin Journal*, 10-13 July 1762; Teerink, *Bibliography of the Writings of Jonathan Swift*, pp. 25, 61.

88. Maty, *Miscellaneous Works*, 4:86 ff.

89. William Cooke, *Memoirs of Samuel Foote*, 1:119.

90. *Boswell's Life of Johnson*, 2:95, 299; see also *Johnsonian Gleanings*, ed. George Birkbeck-Hill (Oxford: Clarendon Press, 1897), 1:424.

91. Gilbert, *History of the City of Dublin*, 2:40.

92. Samuel Foote, *The Orators*.

93. Compare Chesterfield's letters to Faulkner for 17 February 1748 and 4 January 1763; Maty, *Miscellaneous Works*, 4:77, 89.

94. Gilbert, *History of the City of Dublin*, 2:40.

95. Anonymous, "Memoirs of the Late Samuel Foote, Esq.," p. 536.

96. Samuel Foote, "Trial of Samuel Foote, Esq., for the Libel on Peter Paragraph," in Tate Wilkinson's *The Wandering Patentee*, p. 258.

97. Foote, "Trial of Samuel Foote," p. 258n.

98. "Memoirs of the Late Samuel Foote, Esq.," p. 536. In 1766 while on holiday with the Duke of York, Lord Mexborough, and Sir Francis Delaval, Foote fell from his horse. The fracture was so grave

that the surgeon could not mend it; consequently he amputated Foote's leg. The accident so upset the Duke that he helped Foote obtain a perpetual summer patent to the Little Haymarket Theater; Maty, *Miscellaneous Works*, 4:88.

99. Jonathan Swift, *The Works of Dr. Jonathan Swift*, 1:xiv. The small octavo volumes I have seen would fit the Teerink description of the 1766 reprint of the 1760 small octavo. However, the preface would appear to be a reprint of the preface written in 1755 for the quarto and large octavo editions. He does not date the preface; yet he quotes an advertisement by Faulkner in the *Dublin Journal* for 15 October 1754, as if it were a contemporary occurrence.

100. *Prose Works*, 13:203.

101. Teerink, *Bibliography of the Writings of Jonathan Swift*, pp. 25, 38. This Faulkner edition is Teerink #68: I:1763; II:1735; III:1759; IV:1735; V:1738; VI:1738; VII:1751; VIII:1752, IX:1758 X:1762; XI:1763.

102. *Dublin Journal*, 30 April–3 May 1763; 12–15 February 1763; 10–14 July, 24–28 July 1764.

103. *Dublin Journal*, 8–11 June 1765. "George Faulkner, Printer and Bookseller, is removed from the Blind Quay to the Corner of Parliament-street, opposite Essex Bridge and the Custom House. N. B. The best built houses in said Street, next to his with Fronts on said Street are to Let. Inquire of the Printer hereof."

104. [Robert Jephson], *An Epistle to Gorges Edmond Howard*, p. 14n.

105. See supra, Faulkner to O'Conor, 17 November 1767 and 7 November 1766.

106. See supra, Faulkner to O'Conor, n.d. 1768: Memorandum, 19 August 1774.

107. See supra, Faulkner to O'Conor, n.d. 1768.

108. Richard Cumberland, *Memoirs of Richard Cumberland*, p. 174. Faulkner's swallowing "immense potations" of claret might be explained by the following excerpt from John T. Gilbert, "Streets of Dublin," p. 533. "Tis hardly possible, indeed, to make an Irishman, that can in any sense be called a drinker, thoroughly drunk with his claret; by that time he has discharged his five or six bottles, he will get a little flashy, perhaps, and you may drink him to eternity he'll not be much more. One very favourable circumstance for the drinker, custom has here established, their glasses are very small: the largest of these in common use, will not hold more, I believe, than about one-third of a gill, or quartern."

109. 25–28 July 1767.

110. *Dublin Journal*, 8–11 June 1765; 22–25 April 1767; 27 February–1 March 1768. After 1765 Faulkner no longer had control of the remaining Swift material. Volumes fourteen through nineteen are reprints from Hawkesworth and Deane Swift's editions.

111. *Dublin Journal*, 27 February–1 March 1768. Volumes seventeen, eighteen, and nineteen were in the press and were ready for sale possibly by the end of March; Teerink, *Bibliography of the Writings of Jonathan Swift*, p. 47; *Catalogue of the Bradshaw Collection*, 1:195.

112. Teerink, *Bibliography of the Writings of Jonathan Swift*, p. 44. Faulkner advertised in the *Dublin Journal*, 13–16 July 1771, "this

Day is published by the Printer hereof, a compleat Edition of The Works of the Reverend Doctor Jonathan Swift, Dean of St. Patrick's Dublin, in twenty volumes Octavo, price bound 5 £, the same in 20 Volumes, twelves and eighteens, 2 £." This would appear to be a reissue of Teerink #47, with additions printed by Faulkner since 1764.

113. See supra, Faulkner to Derrick, 18 December 1759; O'Conor to Faulkner, 8 August 1763; Faulkner to O'Conor, 7 November 1766; O'Conor to Faulkner, 10 July 1767.

114. *Dublin Journal*, 13–17 September 1737.

115. 29 January–2 February 1745/46.

116. See supra, Faulkner to O'Conor, 3 September 1772.

117. Gilbert, "Streets of Dublin," p. 36.

118. Gilbert, "Streets of Dublin," p. 36; *Catalogue of the Bradshaw Collection*, 1:197.

119. Gilbert, *History of the City of Dublin*, 2:44 ff. Gilbert estimates nine editions of the *Epistle to Gorges Edmond Howard*, but I can count only six – five Dublin editions and one London edition.

120. *Dublin Journal*, 2–5 June 1770.

121. The Newberry Library has copies of both. The lesser known poem was supposed to be Howard's reply to Faulkner: *An Epistle from G-----E-----H---rd, Esq. to Alderman George Faulkner with Notes Explanatory, Critical and Historical by the Alderman and other Learned Authors.*

122. "Monthly Catalogue: Poetical," p. 171.

123. *Dublin Journal*, 10–13 December 1772; 24–26 February 1774. "This Day is published by the Printer Hereof, Letters Written by the Late Right Honourable Philip Stanhope, Earl of Chesterfield, to his Son, Philip Stanhope, Esq., Late Envoy Extraordinary to The Court of Dresden, together with several Other Pieces on various Subjects. Published by Mrs. Eugenia Stanhope. In two volumes. The other Octavo Edition of Lord Chesterfield and Lord Lyttleton's Works elegantly printed on good Paper and in this Type, are also just published by the Printer hereof." This third volume is a mystery since Maty's first edition in 1777 contained only two volumes. Could that third volume have contained Chesterfield's letters to Faulkner?

124. *Dublin Journal*, 22–26 February 1774.

125. "Authentic Memoirs," pp. 569 ff.

126. *Dublin Journal*, 29–31 August 1775.

127. Richard Robert Madden, *The History of Irish Periodical Literature*, 2:47.

Bibliography

PRIMARY SOURCES

Manuscripts

Cambridge, England. Trinity College Library, Cambridge University. Uncataloged manuscript [formerly cataloged in *The Rothschild Library. A Catalogue of Eighteenth Century Printed Books and Manuscripts Formed by Lord Rothschild.* 2 vols. Cambridge: At the University Press, 1954. Vol. 1, p. 201, No. 836].

Cambridge, Mass. Houghton Library, Harvard University. English Ms 218.5, *Orrery Papers,* "A Series of Letters from Ireland."

Dublin. Royal Irish Academy. Ms B-1, B-2.

London. British Museum. Add. Ms 955, 27; Egerton Ms 201, F 31-61.

London. Victoria and Albert Museum. Forster Ms 146, 41-51.

Northampton, England. Fitzwilliam Collection. Northampton Archives Committee, Lamport Hall.

Somerville, N. J. The Hyde Collection.

Printed

Dublin Journal, Irish Newspapers in Dublin Libraries before 1750. Ann Arbor, Mich.: University Microfilms, 1950.

The Dublin Journal and The Freeman's Journal: 1750–1825. Ann Arbor, Mich.: University Microfilms, 1958.

SECONDARY SOURCES

Anonymous. "Authentic Memoirs of the Late George Faulkner, Esq." *Hibernian Magazine* (September 1775): 503–5; (October 1775): 567–71.

————. "A Candid Inquiry into the Causes and Motives of the Late Riots in Munster in Ireland." *Gentleman's Magazine* 27 (1767): 32–34.

Anonymous. "Memoirs of the Late Samuel Foote, Esq." *Gentleman's Magazine* 47 (1777): 441–45.
————. "Monthly Catalogue: Poetical." *Monthly Review* 47 (1772): 171.
Blackstone, William. *Of Public Wrongs.* 2 Vols.: *Commentaries on the Laws of England.* Philadelphia: J. B. Lippencott, 1856.
Boswell, James. *Boswell's Life of Johnson.* Edited by George Birkbeck Hill and Laurence Powell. 6 vols. Oxford: At the Clarendon Press, 1934–1950.
British Museum General Catalogue of Printed Books. 27 vols. London: Trustees of the British Museum, 1955. Reprint. New York: Readex Inc., 1967.
Burke's Genealogical and Heraldic History of the Peerage, Baronetage, and Knightage. London: Shaw, 1938.
Catalogue of the Bradshaw Collection of Irish Books at the University Library, Cambridge. 4 vols. Cambridge: At the University Press, 1916.
Chesterfield, Philip Dormer Stanhope, Earl of. *The Miscellaneous Works of the Late Philip Dormer Stanhope, Earl of Chesterfield.* Edited by Dr. Mathew Maty and John O. Justamond. 4 vols. 2d ed. London: Dilly, 1779.
Clifford, James L. *Young Samuel Johnson.* New York, Toronto and London: McGraw Hill Book Co., 1955.
Collins, A. S. *Authorship in the Days of Samuel Johnson.* New York: Dutton, 1929.
Cooke, William. *Memoirs of Samuel Foote.* London: Richard Phillips, 1805.
Cooper, Anthony Ashley, Third Earl of Shaftesbury. *Characteristics of Men, Manners, Opinions, and Times.* Edited by John M. Robertson. Gloucester, Mass., 1963.
Cornu, Donald. "Swift, Motte, and the Copyright Struggle: Two Unnoticed Documents." *Modern Language Notes* 28(1939): 114–24.
Cumberland, Richard. *Memoirs of Richard Cumberland.* London: Lackington, Allen, 1808.
Delany, Mary. *The Autobiography and Correspondence of Mary Granville, Mrs. Delany.* Edited by Lady Llanover. 2d Ser. London: Richard Bentley, 1861.
Dictionary of National Biography. Edited by Sir Leslie Stephen and Sir Sidney Lee. 27 vols. London: Spottiswoode, 1888–1909. Reprint. London: Oxford University Press, 1921–1922.
Fitzgerald, Brian. "The Earl of Kildare and Archbishop Stone." *Dublin Magazine* 15 (1940): 40–48.
Foote, Samuel. "Mr. Foote's Address to the Public after a Prosecution against Him for Libel." *Gentleman's Magazine* 33 (1763): 39.

————. *The Orators.* London: J. Coote . . . ; G. Kearsley . . . ; T. Davis, London, 1762.

Gilbert, John T. "Correspondence and Mss of Charles O'Conor of Belanagare, County Roscommon." Vol. 7: *Appendix to the Eigthth Report.* London: The Royal Commission on Historical Manuscripts, 1881.

————. *History of the City of Dublin.* 3 vols. Dublin: Mc-Glushan, 1854–1859.

————. "The Streets of Dublin." *Irish Quarterly Review* 2 (September 1852): 494–562.

————. "The Streets of Dublin." *Irish Quarterly Review* 3 (September 1853): 541–625.

Griffith, Reginald H. *Alexander Pope: A Bibliography, 1735–1751.* 2 vols. Austin, Tex.: University of Texas Press, 1922–1927.

Hitchcock, Robert. *Historical View of the Irish Stage.* 2 vols. Dublin: n.p., 1794.

[Jephson, Robert.] *An Epistle to Gorges Edmond Howard, Esq. with Notes Explanatory, Critical and Historical, by George Faulkner, Esq. and Alderman.* Dublin: Wogan, 1771.

Johnson, Samuel. *Johnsonian Gleanings.* Edited by George Birkbeck-Hill. 2 vols. Oxford: At the Clarendon Press, 1897.

————. *Letters of Samuel Johnson.* Edited by R. W. Chapman. 3 vols. Oxford: At the Clarendon Press, 1952.

Knapp, Lewis Mansfield. *Tobias Smollett, Doctor of Men and Manners.* Princeton, N. J.: Princeton University Press, 1949.

Landa, Louis A. *Swift and the Church of Ireland.* 2d ed. Oxford: At the Clarendon Press, 1965.

Lecky, William Edward Hartpole. *A History of Ireland in the Eighteenth Century.* 4 vols. 1892. Reprint. New York: AMS Press, 1969.

London Stage, 1660–1800. Edited by William Van Lennep et al. 11 vols. Carbondale, Ill.: Southern Illinois University Press, 1962–1968.

McKillop, Allen Dugald. *Samuel Richardson: Printer and Novelist.* Chapel Hill, N. C.: University of North Carolina Press, 1936.

Madden, Richard Robert. *The History of Irish Periodical Literature from the End of the Seventeenth Century to the Middle of the Nineteenth Century.* 2 vols. London: Newby, 1867.

Munter, Robert L. *The History of the Irish Newspaper, 1685–1760.* Cambridge: At the University Press, 1967.

Nichols, John. *Literary Anecdotes of the Eighteenth Century Comprizing Biographical Memoirs of William Bowyer, F.S.A. and Many of His Learned Friends. . . .* London: Nichols and Son, 1817.

O'Connor, Charles, S. J. "George Faulkner and the Irish Catholics." *Studies: An Irish Quarterly* 28 (1939): 485–502.

O'Conor, Charles. *Dissertations on a History of Ireland.* Dublin: Faulkner, 1766.

O'Conor, Mathew. *History of the Irish Catholics from the Settlement in 1691, With a View of the State of Ireland from the Invasion of Henry II to the Revolution.* Dublin: n.p., 1813.

Paulson, Ronald. *The Graphic Art of William Hogarth.* 2 vols. New Haven, Conn.: Yale University Press, 1965.

Plomer, H. R., et al. *Dictionary of Printers and Booksellers at Work in England, Scotland and Ireland, 1668–1725.* Oxford: The Bibliographical Society, 1922.

———. *Dictionary of Printers and Booksellers at Work in England, Scotland and Ireland, 1726–1775.* Oxford: The Bibliographical Society, 1932.

Pope, Alexander. *Correspondence of Alexander Pope.* Edited by George Sherburn. 5 vols. Oxford: At the Clarendon Press, 1956.

Richardson, Samuel. *Correspondence of Samuel Richardson.* Edited by Anna Laetitia Barbauld. 6 vols. London, n.p., 1804.

———. *The History of Sir Charles Grandison.* 7 vols. 3d ed. London: Samuel Richardson, 1754.

Smollett, Tobias. *The History of England from the Revolution until the Death of George the Second.* 4 vols. London: n.p., 1812.

[Smollett, Tobias.] "Review of *The Conduct and Treatment of John Crookshank, Esq.*" *Critical Review* 7 (May 1759): 554–57.

———. "Review of *The History of Ireland.*" *Critical Review* 15 (May 1763): 361–67.

Swift, Jonathan. *The Correspondence of Jonathan Swift.* Edited by Harold Williams. 5 vols. Oxford: At the Clarendon Press, 1963–1965.

———. *The Poems of Jonathan Swift.* Edited by Harold Williams. 3 vols. Oxford: At the Clarendon Press, 1956.

———. *The Prose Works of Jonathan Swift.* Edited by Herbert Davis. 14 vols. Oxford: Basil Blackwell at the Shakespeare Head, 1939–1968.

———. *The Works of Dr. Jonathan Swift, Dean of St. Patrick's Dublin.* Edited by John Hawkesworth. London: C. Bathurst et al., 1766.

Teerink, Herman. *Bibliography of the Writings of Jonathan Swift.* Edited by Arthur Scouten. Philadelphia: University of Pennsylvania Press, 1963.

Wilkinson, Tate. *The Wandering Patentee, or The History of the Yorkshire Theatres.* York: n.p., 1794.

Index

Agriculture Law, 103
Anglo-Irish relations: 45, 55, 57, 72 n, 103; provision for Lord Lieutenant, 46 n

Barry, Sir Edward, 21–22
Bowyer, William: letter to, 41
Brooke, Henry, 51 n
Brown, John, 80, 81 n
Burke, Edmund: letter to, 46

Chesterfield, Philip Dormer Stanhope, Earl of, 15, 27; on Faulkner, 16, 22, 23, 24, 125
Clayton, Robert, Bishop of Clogher, 76–77
copyright laws: Bill for the Security of Property in Books, 108; of 1710, 13
Crookshanks, John, 63
Curll, Edmund, 14

Delany, Mary Granville, 17
Derrick, Samuel: edits Dryden's Works, 49; letters to, 49, 54, 56, 61, 63, 66, 67, 69, 70, 73
Dublin, city of: booksellers in, 8; celebrates birthday of George II, 3; prison conditions in, 4; urban problems of, 5
Dublin Society, 32, 119
Dunkin, William, 20, 55, 56 n

Ely, Nicholas Hume, Earl of: trial of, for idiocy, 47–48 n
Ewing, Alexander, 15
Ewing, George, 15

Fairbrother, Samuel, 11
Faulkner, George: early life and career, 6; loses leg, 7; major

competitors of, 7–9, 18, 20; arrested for libel, 9, 12; publishes Swift's collected works, 10, 11, 24, 27, 28, 30, 33, 56; advises Lord Chesterfield, 15; obituary for Swift, 15; compared to Atticus, 16; Richardson accuses, of piracy, 18–20; Kildare persecutes, 21–22; Foote parodies, 24–25; sues Samuel Foote, 26; entertains Lord Lieutenant Townsend, 29; elected high sheriff, 30; elected alderman, 32; feuds with Georges E. Howard, 32–33; death, 34; tombstone inscription, 34; on Irish economy, 44–45, 62; political views of, 74–75, 117; pro-American sentiment of, 117; eulogy, 125
Foote, Samuel: parodies Faulkner, 24–25; sued by Faulkner, 26

Harte, Walter, 51 n
Hoey, James, 7
Hogarth, William: letter to, 37
Hort, Josiah, Bishop of Kilmore, 12
Howard, Georges Edmond, 32–33
Hume, David, 98

Irish history: bibliography of, 59 n–60 n

Jephson, Robert, 28, 33, 121 n
Johnson, Samuel, 77, 78 n, 104

Kildare, James Fitzgerald, Twentieth Earl of, 21–22
Knowles, Charles, 63 n

This book has been set in Linotype Janson,
a recutting of the classic Dutch-style face that
was cast by Nicholas Kis, a 17th-century Hungarian.
The device used on the title page is one that
George Faulkner used in books he printed.

Composition & printing by Heritage Printers, Inc.
Binding by the C.J. Krehbiel Co.
Design by Jonathan Greene

CPSIA information can be obtained
at www.ICGtesting.com
Printed in the USA
BVOW08s2302170418

513674BV00001B/17/P